The Art Of Strategic Resistance

By
Kelly Charles-Collins, Esq., MBA

©2024

ALL RIGHTS RESERVED. No part of this publication may be reproduced, distributed, or transmitted in any form or by any means, including photocopying, recording, or other electronic or mechanical methods, without the prior written permission of the publisher or author, except in the case of brief quotations used in official articles or reviews, provided full attribution is given to the author. Permission for any other use must be obtained directly from the publisher or author.

Published By: Lady Lawyer Media

Paperback ISBN 978-1-7354880-5-9
eBook ISBN 978-1-7354880-6-6

Library of Congress Control Number: 2024925661

PRINTED IN THE UNITED STATES OF AMERICA.

To my beautiful and brilliant Black cousins, Toni Nicole, and Chloé; to my niece, Danielle; and to every other beautiful and brilliant Black woman and girl who feels the weight of the world pressing down and wonders which way to turn. To the warriors like my niece Danielle, who are ready to face the fight, this *Tactical Guide* is for you. May it empower you to rise, resist, and create the life, living, and legacy you desire and deserve.

Contents

Introduction 1

Ode To Our Ancestors 5

The Philosophy of Strategic Resistance:
A Tactical Guide for High-Stakes Times 9

Preface: A Call to Arms. 23

From Fire to Fight: The Next Step in Strategic Resistance 29

Foundation: Be In The Know 31

Marching Orders. 39

Tactical Strategies. 45

Ancestral Legacy and Forward Vision 181

Unyielding Legacy. 185

Built Like My Ancestors: A Battle Cry For The Ages 189

#theartofstrategicresistance

Epilogue..191

Acknowledgments..193

About the Author 195

Strategy Index...197

Introduction

The Art of Strategic Resistance

A Tactical Guide for Leadership, Legacy, and Resilience

Resistance. For many, the word carries a weight, conjuring images of defiance, opposition, or struggle. Yet resistance is much more than that. It is a profound expression of leadership, resilience, and courage. At its core, resistance is the unwavering commitment to stand firm in your values while creating opportunities for growth, progress, and transformation.

Strategic resistance is the art of meeting challenges, not with impulsive reactions, but with clarity, intention, and purpose. It is rooted in knowledge, informed by insight, and fueled by adaptability. It involves the deliberate choice of when, where, how, and why to take action, whether to advance or defend, as circumstances demand.

This Tactical Guide serves as your blueprint for navigating the complexities of high-stakes moments. It is a resource for those ready to lead with courage, act with conviction, and build a legacy of lasting impact. Whether you are a professional seeking to influence decisions, a leader advocating for your team, or an individual striving for personal

#theartofstrategicresistance

growth, the strategies within these pages will equip you to move forward with strength and purpose.

More Than a Tactical Guide: A Universal Tool

While this Tactical Guide was born from my deep desire to empower Black women and girls, those whose brilliance, resilience, and voices have too often been overlooked, it is not limited to them. The principles of strategic resistance are both timeless and universal, designed to meet the needs of anyone facing challenges or stepping into leadership in their personal or professional life.

Much like the enduring wisdom found in the world's greatest strategy texts, this Tactical Guide is crafted to transcend time and context. It equips individuals and organizations with the tools to cultivate clarity, adaptability, and innovation. Whether in a corporate boardroom or a community gathering, making personal decisions, or advancing societal movements, the strategies within these pages provide actionable paths forward for those ready to lead with intention and resilience.

What Strategic Resistance Means

Strategic resistance is not reactionary. It is intentional and proactive. It goes beyond mere opposition, focusing instead on purposeful and thoughtful action. At its core, strategic resistance represents:

- **Insight:** A profound understanding of the game, its rules, the players, and your unique role within it.
- **Adaptability:** The ability to adapt your tactics while remaining true to your core values.

- **Empowered Action:** The courage to move forward with clarity allows us to safeguard what matters most while opening doors for progress.

When approached strategically, resistance becomes a powerful catalyst for transformation. It empowers us to preserve our energy, assert our presence, and shape outcomes with intention and precision.

For Leaders, Visionaries, and Everyday Warriors

This Tactical Guide is for anyone ready to rise in the face of challenge:

- **Corporate Leaders:** Navigate power dynamics, spark innovation, and cultivate lasting influence.
- **Women and Historically Excluded Groups:** Protect your energy, claim your space, and amplify your voice.
- **Visionaries:** Transform doubt into bold action and begin building the future you envision.

Every strategy in this guide is crafted to empower you with the tools to act with clarity and conviction. Whether you're tackling challenges in your workplace, advocating in your community, or navigating personal obstacles, you'll find guidance to help you stand firm while moving forward with purpose.

A Timeless Legacy of Leadership

More than just a Tactical Guide, The Art of Strategic Resistance is a call to action, a resource for growth, and a blueprint for leadership. It

#theartofstrategicresistance

serves as a bridge, connecting the resilience of those who came before us to the legacy we are creating for those who will come after us.

Grounded in the Moment, Built for the Future

While the principles in this Tactical Guide are timeless and its applications universal, it is firmly rooted in the realities of our present world. We find ourselves in high-stakes times, where challenges to freedom, justice, and personal autonomy demand clarity, courage, and decisive action.

As I write, a political climate of uncertainty and fear casts a long shadow. Leadership that prioritizes control over service threatens to unravel democratic norms and restrict hard-won rights. For many, this moment feels heavy with urgency and uncertainty.

This Tactical Guide was created for moments like these. It was born from conversations with those asking the same pressing question: "How do we move forward?" The answer lies not in impulsive reactions but in deliberate strategy. The Art of Strategic Resistance provides tools not only to address today's challenges but also to navigate the complexities of leadership, advocacy, and personal growth, now and in the future.

This is a guide for the present and for what lies ahead.

This is your moment to rise.

To lead.

To resist with intention.

This is The Art of Strategic Resistance.

> *Those who love peace must learn to organize*
> *as effectively as those who love war.*
> Martin Luther King Jr.

#builtlikeourancestors

Ode To Our Ancestors

I often hear people say, "We are our ancestors' wildest dreams." I've also seen the statement, "We are about to see if we are built like our ancestors." My response?

We are Absolutely Built Like Our Ancestors!

This mantra is both the rallying cry for this book and movement and the foundation on which we stand. Within each of us lies the strength of those who came before: those who endured, fought, and rose above unimaginable hardships. Our ancestors didn't just survive; they were warriors in the battle for dignity, freedom, and future generations.

They were built on resilience, fortified by faith, and driven by an unwavering belief that life could be different. That a future of freedom was worth the fight. We stand here today as living proof of their vision. They didn't merely endure; they thrived, they created, they resisted. And they did so with an unbreakable spirit and foresight that transcends time.

Built Like Our Ancestors is more than a rallying cry, it's a reminder. A reminder that their power courses through us, their blood runs within us, and their resilience is ours to wield.

#theartofstrategicresistance

In the face of suffering and injustice, our ancestors found ways to create beauty, nurture joy, build communities, raise families, and dream of a future they might never see. They moved with intention and purpose, refusing to let oppression extinguish their light. They transformed every space they entered, turning pain into power and loss into legacy. This wasn't accidental. It was deliberate. And that same deliberate choice lives in us today.

To be **Built Like Our Ancestors** is to honor their memory, to recognize the battles they fought, and to continue their work with the same fire and faith. They taught us what it means to be unbreakable, compassionate, and fierce defenders of dignity and dreams. Their legacy is not just history. It's our compass, guiding us forward. It's the heartbeat calling us to act, to speak, to resist.

Though we don't face the exact same challenges, the essence of the fight remains. The world has evolved, but oppression adapts, and injustice lingers, testing our strength and resolve, just as it tested theirs. Yet here we are, carrying their legacy forward, knowing that in every challenge and battle, we possess the spirit that overcame far worse.

We are not here simply to survive. We are here to thrive, to build, to create a world that honors our voices, our values, and our ancestors.

To be **Built Like Our Ancestors** is to stand firm, even when the ground shifts beneath our feet. It means holding tight to our vision, even when others try to obscure it. It means wielding our strength with compassion, speaking with purpose, and leading with love, courage, and a vision that reaches far beyond ourselves.

This Tactical Guide is my offering to the future, a way to continue what our ancestors began, to leave our mark, and to ensure that those who come after us will find the path a little clearer, the weight a little lighter, and the resistance a little stronger.

It is for the daughters and sons of warriors, builders, and dreamers. It's for those who understand that our strength doesn't come from easy paths, but from those who carved them out with bare hands, who

#builtlikeourancestors

refused to yield even in the darkest hours. When we say we are **_Built Like Our Ancestors_**, we are claiming a legacy of power that didn't just survive. It thrived, creating art, culture, communities, and families. It's time to carry that power forward, into our own battles, for our own futures.

We are the descendants of those who didn't yield, and we will not yield either.

Let it be known we are here, we're not going anywhere, and **_We are Built Like Our Ancestors._**

The Philosophy of Strategic Resistance: A Tactical Guide for High-Stakes Times

Rooted in strategy but born from a clarion call to every Black woman who's tired of being told to sit down, quiet down, or stand aside. This is your Tactical Guide, crafted to fortify you for every moment when the battle comes to you and to prepare you to take the fight wherever it needs to go.

This is the beginning of a movement, a legacy, a collective force built to endure.

Emotions as Power: Honoring, Harnessing, and Strategizing

In the heat of resistance, we honor our emotions, their fire, their wisdom, their truth. For generations, we've been told to set emotions aside, to make ourselves "acceptable," to stay small. But that's not our way. This plan respects the full spectrum of what we feel, anger, frustration, exhaustion, hope, joy, and shows that these emotions aren't here to hold us back. They're fuel, propelling us forward with purpose.

Yet, Strategic Resistance requires more than just feeling. It demands that we channel those emotions, using them to sharpen our strategies and direct our actions. Here, we move beyond reacting and into responding, staying intentional with every step.

#theartofstrategicresistance

This is your Tactical Guide to navigate each emotion, from righteous anger to unbreakable hope, and turn it into action that aligns with the outcomes you seek.

Resistance as Offense and Defense: A Dual Approach to Power

We're conditioned to think of resistance as defense, as if it's something we do when we're under attack, forced to protect what's already ours. This Tactical Guide equips you to protect what's yours, yes, but it also empowers you to take the offensive when the moment demands. Strategic resistance isn't passive. It's about taking the fight exactly where it needs to go, advancing with intention, seizing the opportunities before us, and asserting our right to claim what's ours.

Offensive resistance is about stepping into your full power. It's about asserting your rights without waiting for permission, advancing with purpose, and making the moves that matter. But this Tactical Guide is not about recklessness. It's about being ready. It prepares you to hold your ground and take the lead, not because you need validation, but because you're built for this.

Preparedness as Power

Preparation is the key. Too often, we charge into battles unprepared, driven by emotion but lacking a plan. This Tactical Guide offers the clarity to pause, prepare, and move forward with purpose. Whether the challenge is one you anticipated or one that caught you off guard, this guide provides a structured approach rooted in your values, reinforced by strategy, and adaptable to changing circumstances.

Strategic resistance isn't about recklessness. It's about readiness. This Tactical Guide serves as your anchor, helping you stay focused and

#builtlikeourancestors

composed when the stakes are high. Designed to support you at every step, it's a blueprint you can evaluate, refine, and rely on. With this guide, you'll be empowered to protect your space and push boundaries intentionally and strategically, staying true to your values and purpose.

Preparedness provides the foundation, but power is amplified when paired with clarity about who you are and how you engage with the world. It's not enough to have a plan; you need a guiding framework that aligns your actions with your purpose. This is where the V Suite™ comes in, a dynamic compass to ground your strategy and propel your resistance.

The V Suite: Vision, Voice, Visibility, and Value™

Strategic resistance starts with a solid foundation, a clear understanding of who you are, what you stand for, and how you choose to engage with the world. At the core of this Tactical Guide is the V Suite™: four interconnected pillars designed to empower you to lead with purpose, navigate pivotal moments, and build a legacy that lasts.

The pillars—Vision, Voice, Visibility, and Value—serve as the cornerstone of your leadership and resistance. Together, they provide a framework to reclaim your power, amplify your presence, and align your actions with your deepest purpose.

Vision: The Clarity to See Beyond the Immediate

Vision is about understanding where you're going and why. It's the ability to cut through the noise and distractions, focusing on what truly matters. Vision allows you to chart a course that stays true to your values and aligns with your goals.

Ask yourself: What am I working toward? How does this align with my broader purpose?

#theartofstrategicresistance

Voice: The Courage to Speak Your Truth

Your voice is your superpower. It's the tool you use to advocate for yourself and others, confront injustice, and inspire meaningful change. When you speak with clarity and conviction, your message resonates deeply and has the potential to shape outcomes.

    Ask yourself: What needs to be said? How can I use my voice to create impact?

Visibility: The Intentional Choice to Show Up

Visibility is about choosing to step forward and claim your space. It's the courage to stand tall in environments where you may have been overlooked or underestimated, ensuring your contributions are acknowledged and your presence is undeniable.

    Ask yourself: How can I show up fully and authentically? What space is mine to claim?

Value: The Unshakable Understanding of Your Worth

Value is the cornerstone of it all, a profound belief in your worth and a commitment to ensuring it is honored. It's understanding that you "belong everywhere you are, but you don't belong everywhere." It's recognizing that your contributions matter and that you are deserving of respect and recognition.

    Ask yourself: Am I honoring my own value? How do I ensure others do the same?

#builtlikeourancestors

A Framework for Action

The V Suite™ is more than a philosophy. It's a call to action. Each strategy in this Tactical Guide is designed to strengthen your Vision, amplify your Voice, increase your Visibility, and reinforce your Value. Whether you're standing firm in the face of adversity, rallying allies to a cause, or holding others accountable, these pillars ensure that every step you take is intentional and aligned.

When you lead from your V Suite™, you are unstoppable. You become a force of nature, unyielding, unapologetic, and ready to navigate any challenge with confidence and clarity. These four pillars are not just tools: they're a way of life. They guide you to lead, resist, and rise with purpose.

Your V Suite™ in Action

Think of the V Suite™ as your compass. Let it inspire you to dream boldly, speak truthfully, show up fearlessly, and demand your due. When you align your Vision, Voice, Visibility, and Value, there's nothing you cannot achieve.

As you explore the strategies in this Tactical Guide, reflect on how each one connects to the V Suite™. Where does it strengthen your Vision, amplify your Voice, enhance your Visibility, or affirm your Value? By intentionally applying these pillars, you can tailor your battle plan to meet your goals and fortify your leadership in every moment.

This is how we lead. This is how we resist. This is how we win.

For Black Women, By a Black Woman

To my sisters: This Tactical Guide was written with you in mind. I know the sting of being doubted, dismissed, and diminished, and I

#theartofstrategicresistance

know the triumph of rising anyway. Every word in this guide is here to remind you that your voice holds power, your presence radiates strength, and your resistance is essential.

This is more than a collection of strategies. It's a path forward, rooted in resilience and designed to honor the warrior within. Together, we will face high-stakes moments with courage, conviction, and clarity, not because it's easy, but because it's our right.

Leading From the Front: Our Call to Lead

Black women have always led, from the shadows, from the sidelines, and, when the moment demanded it, from the front. Leadership isn't defined by titles or roles. It's about how we show up, how we move, and how we inspire others to rise with us. Today, more than ever, Black women leading from the front isn't just important, it's essential.

Whether you're managing a team, running a business, raising a family, or simply navigating the world with your head held high, you are a leader. You set the tone. You influence outcomes. You create legacies. Don't let anyone tell you otherwise. The world may not always give us the recognition we deserve, but leadership is about action, not accolades.

In this moment, Black women are called to lead with courage, vision, and unshakable determination. We must claim our power to shape decisions, challenge injustices, and create spaces that honor our value and amplify our voices. We are not waiting for permission to lead. We are taking the reins. The stakes are too high to stand back, and we were never built for the sidelines.

Leadership means forging paths where none exist. It means speaking out when others stay silent. It's about building community, fostering change, and ensuring the next generation has more opportunities than we ever imagined. Whether in boardrooms, classrooms, or living rooms, we lead because we must. We lead because we can.

#builtlikeourancestors

As you reflect on this, ask yourself: Where can I lead from the front in my life? How will I answer the call? Leadership isn't about perfection. It's about purpose and power. And leading with purpose and power is what Black women do best.

We are **Built Like Our Ancestors**, leaders in every sense of the word. The question isn't whether we're ready to lead. The question is: *Where will we lead next?*

Individual and Collective Power: The Strength in Both

In every fight, there's strength in standing alone and power in standing together. The Art of Strategic Resistance honors both, recognizing that each path carries its own purpose and potency. This Tactical Guide is about knowing when to stand independently and when to strategically align with others. It's about joining forces or gathering in numbers with intention.

We understand that, for some, the idea of joining a collective can feel uncertain, especially in a world where trust and integrity are precious and, at times, rare. That trepidation is valid, and discernment is a critical part of this journey.

The fear of aligning with the wrong people or compromising your values is real, and it's wise to heed that instinct. True collective power doesn't come from joining every movement or following every voice. It comes from aligning with purpose, choosing connections that uplift and empower. This guide encourages you to ask yourself:

- Do these alliances resonate with my goals?
- Do they strengthen my resolve?
- Do they respect my boundaries and align with my morals and values?

#theartofstrategicresistance

By cultivating discernment, you're not closing yourself off to others; you're ensuring that when you stand together, you're truly standing in power.

Individual power is not diminished by collective strength. In fact, some of the strongest acts of resistance come from solitary decisions—saying no, walking away, or challenging injustice. These quiet yet profound choices shape our lives and demonstrate the power of conviction. This guide equips every woman to fight her own battles, knowing her individual courage forms a foundation others can lean on, even when her fight goes unseen.

Yet, as powerful as our individual choices are, there is a force that only grows when we come together. Collective power multiplies our voices and amplifies our impact. When we align with those who share our values and vision, we become unstoppable.

This Tactical Guide celebrates both the strength of unity and the power of discernment. It's a reminder that no one fights alone: each act of individual courage strengthens the whole, and each collective stand fuels our individual resolve. This is resistance that respects both the singular and the collective, rooted in strategy, guided by purpose, and elevated by intentionality.

The Power of Collabosourcing®: Strength in Unity

In times like these, our strength lies both in what we can achieve individually and what we can build together. For too long, we've been conditioned to see each other as competition instead of allies. We've been told there's only so much space at the table, and that if one of us wins, another must lose. That lie has robbed us of the transformative power of collaboration.

But now, more than ever, we must reject that mindset.

This is not a moment to compete. This is a moment to collabosource.

#builtlikeourancestors

Collabosourcing® is about leveraging our collective expertise, resources, and relationships to elevate our businesses, brands, and badassery, not to tear each other down, but to lift each other up. It's about understanding that no single table, no single leader, no single perspective holds all the answers. It's about bringing your table to mine, combining strengths, and creating something far greater than either of us could build alone.

It's about asking:

- What unique strengths do I bring to the table that can uplift others?
- Where can I grow by learning from someone else's expertise?
- How can I lead boldly in my areas of strength while following humbly where I need guidance?

Collabosourcing® reminds us that leadership isn't always about standing in front. Sometimes, it's about standing beside or even behind. It's about supporting the person who's leading today while preparing the next leader to step forward tomorrow.

This is the moment for us to unite as a collective, to collaborate, create, disrupt, and dismantle. It's a call to lean on one another, learn from one another, and leverage each other's brilliance to spark the kind of change that endures for generations.

The truth is no one navigates high-stakes moments alone. We need each other. We need to shift our mindset from seeing each other as competition to recognizing each other as collaborators. Together, we must embrace the reality that our shared purpose is far more powerful than any individual agenda.

Our motto is simple: We don't compete. We collabosource.

When we embrace this mindset, we not only lead from the front, but we also clear the path for those who follow to lead with even greater power and purpose.

#theartofstrategicresistance

Building a Legacy Through Collaboration

When we choose to collabosource, we're doing more than supporting each other in the present. We're building a legacy of unity, resilience, and power for generations to come. Every time we share knowledge, amplify each other's voices, or create something together, we shift the narrative for Black women and girls everywhere.

This isn't just about overcoming today's challenges. It's about shaping tomorrow. The tables we build now will be the ones our daughters, nieces, mentees, and sisters stand at, and they'll know how to lead and collaborate because they've seen us do it first.

Collabosourcing® is an act of resistance. It's a declaration that we will not be divided, diminished, or dismissed. It lays the foundation for a future where every voice, every contribution, and every hand lifted in support drives the movement for lasting change.

This is how we win. Together.

Movement Over Moment: The Art of Strategic Resistance

The Art of Strategic Resistance is not a reaction to a single event. It's a long-term commitment, a movement grounded in resilience, awareness, and collective strength. While moments may ignite action, a true movement sustains it. Too often, we've witnessed brief flashes of unity, bursts of rage, and calls to action that fade before they can create lasting change. This Tactical Guide was designed to break that cycle.

This is about more than immediate results. It's about the slow, steady work of transformation, one decision at a time, one voice at a time, one sister at a time.

This movement isn't here to capture the urgency of a single season or react to a specific moment. We're not rising only when it's trending. We're building a foundation that withstands every twist, every challenge,

#builtlikeourancestors

every triumph, and every setback. Strategic resistance acknowledges that while some moments demand immediate action, true change is forged in sustained effort. This guide is a blueprint, not just for high-stakes times but for all the times in between.

Here, we don't just speak to respond; we prepare to endure. We act knowing that others will join, that those who resist injustice and fight to be heard are part of a movement far bigger than any one individual.

The Art of Strategic Resistance is about momentum, not just action. It's the beginning of something enduring. Something each of us will shape, carry, and pass on, transforming not only ourselves but the world we leave behind.

Our Rallying Cry: Built Like Our Ancestors

This movement isn't a passing trend or a fleeting moment. The Art of Strategic Resistance is rooted in a legacy that has withstood the test of time. When we declare, **Built Like Our Ancestors**, we invoke a history of resilience, fierce determination, and unwavering courage in the face of oppression. Our ancestors didn't endure, create, and thrive because it was easy. They did it because they had no other choice. They laid the foundation of resistance upon which we now stand, gifting us the strength to continue the fight as both protectors and warriors in our own lives.

But this is more than a tribute to our history. It's a rallying cry for today's resistance. When you affirm that you're Built Like Our Ancestors, you are claiming the indomitable power within you. The part that refuses to yield, that adapts, survives, and most importantly, rises. It's a declaration of deep respect for those who came before us and a commitment to those who will come after. We are choosing to embody their resilience, ingenuity, and courage, not just through words, but through deliberate action.

#theartofstrategicresistance

This rallying cry also serves as a call to share and amplify our collective strength. Taking up this mantle isn't just about personal empowerment; it's about building and fortifying the power of our community. Resistance, when shared, transforms from an individual effort into an unstoppable force. Let **Built Like Our Ancestors** guide your steps, shape your strategies, and deepen your commitment to this fight. Let it be the anthem that connects you to your roots and unites us all in a shared purpose, a rallying war cry for freedom, agency, and resilience.

This isn't just a message to hold close; it's one to spread far and wide. Share this Tactical Guide. Pass it along to those who need it. Every copy shared, every conversation sparked, and every community engaged becomes an act of resistance in itself.

To bring these strategies to life, pair this guide with The Art of Strategic Resistance Battle Planner, available at www.theartofstrategicresistance.com. Designed to help you create and track your personalized battle plan, the Battle Planner is your companion for turning insight into action, ensuring that you achieve success every step of the way.

Together, we are creating a movement built on legacy, strength, and an unwavering commitment to never back down. This is the beginning of a new chapter in our collective power. A testament to both the strength of those who came before us and the choices we make to honor them today.

The Outcome: Empowerment, Freedom & Self-Defined Victory

The vision for this Tactical Guide isn't a one-size-fits-all solution. For some, the goal is empowerment; for others, it's freedom, inner peace, or reclaiming agency over their lives. Each of us carries a unique

#builtlikeourancestors

vision of victory, and this guide honors that individuality. Your path, your vision, and your outcomes are yours to define.

In every moment, this Tactical Guide helps you set your intentions and align your objectives, allowing you to make decisions from a place of clarity, not fear. Your victory doesn't need to mirror anyone else's. It's defined by what matters most to you.

As you move through these strategies, you'll learn to ground your actions in clear intentions. Ask yourself: What am I fighting for? What's my purpose? What emotion is driving me? By answering these questions, you'll not only clarify your objectives but also identify the strategies best suited to create your vision of success.

We are *Built Like Our Ancestors*!

#theartofstrategicresistance

Preface: A Call to Arms

They Brought the War to Us

This Tactical Guide is my way of fighting back. It's rooted in real conversations and moments I can't ignore. This isn't about a single policy or headline; it's about the 2024 election and everything it represents for us as women. The divisiveness, the hatred, the outright threats against everything we've fought so hard to protect. They're not even hiding their intentions anymore. They're openly, proudly aiming to strip away our power, to make us feel powerless. But feeling powerless is not the same as being powerless. This Tactical Guide is for every woman who feels like there's no way forward, because I know there is. It's also for every woman who knows there's a way forward and is prepared to fight.

It started with a message from my cousin, Toni Nicole. She posted on Facebook that she wasn't okay, that she was sad and terrified. Seeing her words, I immediately reached out to check on her. Her response was simple and raw: "I'm not okay." When I called, I could hear the weight of defeat in her voice. Her words were filled with fear and frustration: "What are we supposed to do? Are we even going to be able to vote anymore?"

Toni Nicole is a millennial, a young woman working hard to build her life, and yet here she was, feeling like she had no agency, no way to

#theartofstrategicresistance

impact what seemed inevitable. Her fear wasn't just about one election; it was about losing her power to shape her future. And I know so many women feel the same way.

Then there's my younger cousin, Chloé. Her father, David, shared a message in our family's WhatsApp group, saying she had come to him crying. Later that day, I texted her to check in and see how she was feeling. Her response? "It's been a rough day, but maybe tomorrow will be a new day."

Chloé is a college student, part of Gen Z, and like so many young women her age, she's been deeply impacted by this moment. She's hurt and upset, wrestling with what this all means for her future. And yet, despite her sadness, she's holding onto a thread of hope, a belief that tomorrow can look different. That hope is everything. It's what keeps us moving forward, even when everything feels stacked against us.

And then there's my niece Danielle. She's a millennial and a lawyer who's completely battle-ready. Fired up and ready to go, she's the one who says, "fuck around and find out." And dare I say, she got that fire from her auntie, ME.

These three young women, Toni, feeling the weight of defeat; Chloé, clinging to hope; and Danielle, fueled and ready to fight, represent the very real impact of this moment. They come from a family of fighters, yet even in a family like ours, some are grappling with despair and uncertainty. For me, hearing the struggles of two women in my own family was a call to action I couldn't ignore.

This Tactical Guide had to be written, not just for them, but for every woman who feels the weight of this moment. It's also for those like Danielle, who are ready to fight but need the right tools in their arsenal to do so effectively.

These three women embody the spectrum of emotions so many of us feel in the face of loss or uncertainty. But no matter where you find yourself, defeated, hopeful, or battle-ready, your response requires intention and strategy.

#builtlikeourancestors

A Moment I'll Never Forget

These conversations took me back to the night Hillary Clinton lost the election. I remember the crushing weight of that moment, the disbelief, the anger, the sorrow. I shared those feelings openly on what was then Twitter (now X, or whatever it's called by the time you're reading this). The next day, my boss called, not to offer support or acknowledge the pain I felt, but to question why I was tweeting about it. It was as if my voice, my feelings, didn't matter. He insisted I delete my tweets, claiming they could harm the firm. Reluctantly, I complied. But I vowed then and there: I would never silence myself like that again.

That moment has stayed with me, a painful reminder of the pressure to remain quiet, to accept things as they are, to avoid rocking the boat. But that's not who I am, and it's not who I'm asking you to be.

Our Strength Lies in Unity and Purpose

In moments like these, we must remember that our power comes not only from our resilience but also from our unity. There will always be forces that try to define us, limit us, or strip us of agency. But we are the ones who decide what we will accept and how we will fight back. Righteous resistance, persistence, and resilience must guide us. This is not just about surviving the challenges we face. It's about wielding our collective power, building coalitions, and ensuring that our voices are heard, and our presence felt.

Even when the odds seem insurmountable, even when all hope feels lost, we still have agency. We still have strength and fortitude. As Queen Bey reminds us: "This that war. This that bloodline on the frontline, ready for war." That strength is in our bloodline; it's in our DNA. We hold the power to make choices, to take decisive action, and to change the course of events. When the path forward seems unclear, remember

#theartofstrategicresistance

this: the ability to influence outcomes, shift perspectives, and create meaningful change lies within us. We're not waiting for permission to lead. We're choosing to lead, with grit and with grace.

In these critical moments, we become architects of our own resilience, standing firm, and moving forward with a strength no one can take from us.

Speaking Up, Speaking Out

We have to speak up and speak out. We cannot allow others to define who we are or silence what we stand for. Together, we have the power to challenge injustice, set the agenda, and craft a vision for a better future. One that uplifts our communities and creates lasting change.

Resilience means refusing to back down, even when the odds are against us. It means summoning the courage to keep pushing forward, knowing that every step we take can inspire others to do the same. This moment demands that we each take responsibility, not to accept what's handed to us but to shape what comes next.

Let's decide, here and now, that we won't be silent. Let's choose to lead with purpose and intention. Together, we have the strength to face whatever comes, to rise above it, and to create a future that reflects our values and aspirations.

My Promise to Every Woman

We're in a new kind of war. They've brought the fight to us and, in their arrogance, handed us their playbook, Project 2025, 900 pages of exactly what they plan to do. They think we're too distracted by their moves to make our own. But they're wrong. We have a choice: to lay down and die or to strategically resist.

#builtlikeourancestors

Preface: A Call to Arms

I've dedicated my life to strategy, to high-stakes engagement, and now I'm channeling everything I know into this fight, for Toni Nicole, for Chloé, for Danielle, and for every woman who feels exhausted, uncertain, worn down by the bullshit, yet ready to fight.

This is not about pretending the pain isn't real or suppressing what you feel. Your fear, anger, and heartbreak are valid. You deserve space to feel it all. But don't stay there. That's what they hope for. That we'll stay paralyzed in our pain, too defeated to move. I refuse to let them win, and I refuse to let you believe that's all we can do.

This Tactical Guide Is My Stand

I can't and won't let this moment pass without taking a stand. This is not about just "getting through." It's about stepping up, equipping every woman who reads this with the mindset, strategies, and courage to rise, to reclaim her space, to say: "I'm here, and I'm not backing down."

The strategies I'm offering aren't abstract theories. They're rooted in lived experiences, battle-tested for the moments when the stakes are high, the pressure is on, and every move matters. This is your guide to stepping into your power with purpose and precision.

To Toni Nicole, Chloé, Danielle, and every woman feeling the weight of this moment, hear this: We are more powerful than they think. We are not just soldiers. We are warriors. And this fight is far from over.

We ride at dawn ...

We Are **Built Like Our Ancestors**!

Kelly

#theartofstrategicresistance

From Fire to Fight: The Next Step in Strategic Resistance

You've tapped into the well of your power, a power deeply rooted in the legacy of those who came before you. You've reclaimed the strength, clarity, and conviction that flows through your veins. A foundation upon which your resistance is built.

But reflection without action is incomplete. Legacy without movement is just a dream.

This next section is where strategy meets execution. It's where we turn purpose into power, dreams into direction, and conviction into conquest. This is where the warrior in you steps forward, ready to act with intention, clarity, and unshakable focus.

We move from heart to hands. From words to work. From inspiration to impact.

The strategies ahead are your tools, carefully forged for the high-stakes battles you face, whether on the front lines of your community, in corporate workplaces, or in those moments where your voice insists on being heard. These are not abstract ideas. They are actionable steps, built for the realities you navigate and tailored for the resistance you lead.

Take this moment. Breathe deeply. Ground yourself. Prepare.

#theartofstrategicresistance

The time to fight is now.

And as you step into the strategies that follow, remember: you are not simply moving through the world. You are moving the world.

#builtlikeourancestors

CHAPTER 1

FOUNDATION: BE IN THE KNOW

A Warrior's First Command: Know Yourself

Before entering any space, whether it's a boardroom, an online forum, a negotiation, or even a written exchange, every warrior must adhere to one essential command: Be In The Know. This principle grounds every action we take, equipping us with self-awareness, clarity, and purpose to move with unwavering intention. When we know ourselves, understand the landscape, and align our actions with our values, we harness an undeniable strength.

In this Tactical Guide, to Be In The Know means approaching every moment, digital or physical, with fierce focus and readiness. We live in an age where battles are no longer confined to face-to-face encounters; they unfold in emails, on social media, and across online platforms where the stakes are equally high.

The strategies that follow are designed to prepare you for any space where you choose to show up, where your voice is heard, your presence felt, and your impact made.

The Eight Keys to Being In The Know

1. KNOW THE GAME

- **What It Means:** Every space, whether it's a meeting room, a digital platform, or a written exchange, operates with its own dynamics and rules. Understanding the purpose, tone, and atmosphere of each environment gives you a critical advantage. Are you stepping into a public discussion, a private negotiation, or a structured debate? Knowing the context allows you to engage with precision and purpose.

- **How to Use It:** Before stepping into any space, ask yourself: What is the purpose of this room, page, or platform? What does this

#builtlikeourancestors

environment require, and how can I approach it on my terms? When you understand the dynamics at play, you position yourself to navigate them effectively, adapting your strategy to meet the moment with confidence and control.

2. **KNOW THE PLAYERS**

- **What It Means:** Understand who occupies the space, whether they are physically present, following along silently, or contributing to a digital community. Pay attention to their roles - key influencers, vocal supporters, and quiet onlookers – the motivations, and the underlying power dynamics. Knowing who holds influence or where alliances may form provides clarity, helping you navigate with confidence and foresight.

- **How to Use It:** Observe and assess the room, whether it's a physical gathering or an online interaction. Identify who holds influence? Who is actively engaging, and who is silently observing? Analyze their motivations and alignments to anticipate your moves, refine your approach, and position yourself effectively within the environment.

3. **KNOW THE RULES**

- **What It Means**: Every environment operates within a framework of unspoken norms, a rhythm of how things are done. This applies to online platforms, written exchanges, and in-person spaces alike, where language, tone, and protocol can differ greatly. Understanding these unwritten rules helps you avoid missteps and equips you with a blueprint to engage effectively.

- **How to Use It:** Take note of the tone, behavior, and communication styles present in the space. Is this an environment where formality

#theartofstrategicresistance

and structure are the norms, or is openness and candor more common? Are interactions driven by strict guidelines, or is there room for flexibility? By understanding the rules, you gain the power to decide when to follow them and when to disrupt them, strategically and with purpose, whether you're navigating a comment thread, a conference call, or a community meeting.

4. KNOW YOUR ROLE

- **What It Means:** Are you stepping into this space as a leader, an advisor, a supporter, an advocate, or an observer? Every role carries its own kind of power when approached with clarity and confidence. Understanding your role ensures that your contributions are purposeful and impactful.

- **How to Use It:** Before engaging, ground yourself in your role. Whether you're standing up for yourself, amplifying someone else's voice, or lending support, move with intention. A warrior recognizes their role and fully embraces it, whether they're leading the charge, holding the line, or championing a cause.

5. KNOW YOUR VALUE

- **What It Means:** You are not here by chance. Your voice, your perspective, and your experiences are uniquely yours, and they matter. When you know your value, you stand on a foundation of self-assurance, allowing you to speak and act with conviction in any space.

- **How to Use It**: Before stepping into action, take a moment to affirm what makes you essential in this moment. What do you

#builtlikeourancestors

bring to the table that no one else does? Knowing your value means embracing your strengths unapologetically, whether in a face-to-face conversation or through a digital interaction.

6. **KNOW YOUR MISSION**

   - **What It Means:** Clarity of purpose is your anchor when distractions or resistance threaten to derail you. Whether you're engaging online or in person, knowing your mission ensures that every word and action aligns with your highest goals.

   - **How to Use It:** Step into each space with your mission firmly in mind. Ask yourself: What is my purpose here? What's worth fighting for? Let these answers guide you, whether you're participating in a meeting, joining a conversation, or navigating a message board. A warrior knows their mission and remains unwavering in their pursuit of it.

7. **KNOW YOUR LIMITS**

   - **What It Means:** Recognizing and respecting your physical, mental, and emotional boundaries is key to sustainable resistance. Knowing your limits isn't a sign of weakness. It's an act of strength. It means understanding when to pause, rest, or delegate, ensuring that you can continue to fight effectively over the long haul.

   - **How to Use It**: Regularly check in with yourself. Assess your energy levels, capacity, and well-being. Before committing to new challenges or pushing through tough moments, ask if this aligns with your current state and long-term goals. Build a habit of self-awareness to prevent burnout. By respecting your limits, you protect your resilience and ensure you're always ready for what's next.

#theartofstrategicresistance

8. **KNOW THE ENDGAME**

   - **What It Means:** Defining your desired outcome provides focus and direction. Whether in a physical space or online, every move you make should serve your ultimate goal. Knowing your endgame keeps you centered, ensuring that your efforts bring meaningful results.

   - **How to Use It:** Envision the impact you want to leave behind. Consider: How do I want others to feel when I leave the room, log off, or sign my name? Let this vision shape your approach, keeping you purposeful and aligned. With your endgame in mind, you move with intention, always prioritizing what truly matters.

Applying "Be In The Know" Across All Spaces

This Tactical Guide extends far beyond the walls of conference rooms or the spotlight of public speaking stages. In today's interconnected world, our battles often unfold online, through emails, social media threads, and written spaces where our voices carry undeniable weight. Each strategy within this guide calls you to Be In The Know, to ground yourself in the essential keys that prepare you to step into any arena, ready to engage wherever the fight takes you.

When you internalize these eight keys as part of your warrior mindset, you move beyond merely following strategies, you embody them. You show up with fierce focus and unwavering intention, whether face-to-face or through the written word. This is where your power ignites. This is where strategy begins.

With the foundation of Being in the Know firmly in place, it's time to transform that awareness into decisive action. These keys equip you

#builtlikeourancestors

with clarity and purpose as you face every situation. But clarity, while essential, is only the beginning.

To navigate the high-stakes terrain ahead, you need principles that anchor your every move, a code to live by, guiding you in both preparation and practice. These are your marching orders: a powerful set of directives to sharpen your focus, fuel your determination, and ensure that every step forward is deliberate, strategic, and rooted in your strength.

CHAPTER 2

MARCHING ORDERS

In times of challenge, these Marching Orders serve as your guideposts, principles that shape not only the actions you take but the legacy you leave behind. Each directive is a clear and grounding statement, crafted to help you navigate moments when strategic resistance is required. These are not lofty ideals; they are actionable principles that have guided leaders, visionaries, and changemakers throughout history.

These Marching Orders are for the moments when uncertainty, exhaustion, or isolation creep in. They echo timeless values, resilience, leadership, courage, and the strength of collective action, that empower you to rise with clarity and purpose. Together, they create a framework for navigating high-stakes situations with intention, grounded in values that endure through adversity.

Why They Matter

Strategic resistance is both an art and a discipline. These orders embody principles that connect you to a broader legacy of strength, adaptability, and unwavering commitment to causes greater than yourself. They matter because they shift your mindset, from reacting to circumstances to reshaping them. Each one reminds you that every decision, every action, and every stand you take can be a meaningful step toward lasting change.

How to Use Them

The Marching Orders are your resource to draw on when you need guidance, whether you're in the midst of an intense negotiation, rallying allies, or standing your ground. Organized around themes such as leadership, resilience, coalition-building, and legacy, they offer practical insight tailored to the challenges you face.

#builtlikeourancestors

Use them as preparation before entering a pivotal moment, as a reference when evaluating your next steps, or as daily affirmations to align your thoughts and actions with your vision. They are not static rules but tools to help you embody these principles, not just in one defining moment, but in the many decisions that together create your impact.

What They Offer

These Marching Orders guide you to act with strength, wisdom, and intention. They remind you that in The Art of Strategic Resistance, true power lies in clarity, purpose, and the courage to forge your own path.

This is your call to action. Ground yourself in these principles, and step forward with the confidence that your resistance is not just necessary. It is transformative.

How They Work Together with the Strategies

While the strategies in this Tactical Guide provide specific actions for navigating high-stakes moments, these Marching Orders serve as broader guiding principles, statements of purpose that frame the mindset behind every action. Think of them as the foundation upon which strategies are built. They give meaning to each tactic, ensuring your intentions remain clear and grounded.

Where strategies help you respond to immediate challenges or achieve defined goals, the Marching Orders act as a steadying force, anchoring you in core values. They remind you of the resilience, adaptability, and courage required to make each strategy uniquely your own. Together, they empower you to move forward with clarity and conviction, ensuring alignment between your actions and the legacy you are building.

#theartofstrategicresistance

1. **Leadership and Vision**
   - Lead with Intention and Integrity: Ground every action in your purpose, ensuring your decisions not only inspire but also drive meaningful results. Let your integrity be the foundation that strengthens your influence.
   - Set the Tone, Then Step Aside: Establish a clear vision, inspire action, and empower others to rise by leaning into their unique strengths. Leadership isn't about control. Rather, it's about fostering trust and collaboration.
   - Be Unyielding in Your Vision: Keep your goals sharp and unwavering, especially when faced with obstacles. Challenges are inevitable, but clarity and focus will guide you through them with strength and resolve.

2. **Resilience and Perseverance**
   - Turn Pain into Power: Use setbacks as fuel to propel your journey forward. Every challenge holds the potential to strengthen your resolve.
   - Rest, but Never Retreat: Take time to recharge and protect your well-being, but never abandon the mission. Rest is preparation, not surrender.
   - Stand Steady in Your Convictions: Stay firmly rooted in your values. Let them anchor and guide you through even the toughest adversities.

3. **Coalition-Building and Allies**
   - Unite Around Shared Purpose: Forge alliances with those who align with your vision and values, creating a unified front grounded in shared goals.

#builtlikeourancestors

- Build Trust Through Transparency: Cultivate open communication and foster accountability to create stronger, more resilient relationships.
- Honor Every Voice: Embrace the power of diverse perspectives, recognizing that collective wisdom is a source of strength and innovation.

4. Strategic Action and Initiative
- Act with Precision, Not Impulse: Approach every move with intentionality, ensuring it aligns with your long-term goals. Thoughtful action beats reaction every time.
- Leverage the Power of Surprise: Unpredictability is a weapon. Use it strategically to disrupt expectations and maintain the upper hand.
- Balance Caution with Boldness: Understand when to take calculated risks and when restraint serves the bigger picture. Knowing when to push forward and when to pause is the key to sustaining momentum.

5. Adaptability and Flexibility
- Pivot with Purpose: Adapt your approach as needed, but never lose sight of your ultimate goals. Flexibility paired with clarity ensures progress.
- Learn and Evolve in Real Time: View challenges as opportunities to grow stronger, wiser, and more capable in the moment.
- Hold Your Vision, Adjust Your Steps: Stay unwavering in your destination, but remain agile and open to shifting paths along the way.

6. Self-Mastery and Discipline
- Command Yourself First: True influence begins with mastering your own thoughts, actions, and emotions. Lead yourself before leading others.

#theartofstrategicresistance

- Guard Your Energy: Focus your efforts on battles that align with your mission. Conserve your energy for what truly matters.
- Practice Patience as a Strength: Patience is not passive; it's a deliberate act of strength that sustains you as you work toward meaningful outcomes.

7. **Preparation and Readiness**
   - Equip Yourself with Knowledge: Stay informed, aware, and ready to face any challenge head-on. Knowledge is your most versatile tool.
   - Organize Your Resources: Identify your strengths, tools, and allies, and deploy them strategically to maximize impact.
   - Anticipate Possible Outcomes: Hope for success but prepare for setbacks. Planning for multiple scenarios keeps you grounded and adaptable.

From Orders to Action: Your Next Move

Now that you've received your marching orders, you're equipped with principles to ground you, guide you, and inspire you. But principles alone are not enough. They need action to bring them to life.

This next section is where the real work begins. It's time to roll up your sleeves and move from mindset to motion, from inspiration to implementation. These strategies are your arsenal, designed to help you navigate high-stakes moments, protect your peace, and take bold, intentional action.

Before we dive into the strategies, let's make sure you're clear on how to use them effectively.

Ready? Let's get to it.

#builtlikeourancestors

CHAPTER 3

TACTICAL STRATEGIES

1.	Devise Your Strategy	53
2.	Ponder and Deliberate	57
3.	Stand Your Ground	61
4.	Scout the Terrain	65
5.	Exploit the Gap	69
6.	Position for Power	73
7.	Develop Your Playbook	77
8.	Command the Room	81
9.	Speak with Purpose	85
10.	Rally Your Allies and Advocates	89
11.	Organize, Mobilize, Engage	93
12.	Engage the Opposition	99
13.	Speak Truth to Power	103
14.	Engage the Disengaged	109
15.	Challenge with Conviction	113
16.	Disrupt Expectations	119
17.	Demand Accountability	123
18.	Execute with Precision	127
19.	Leverage and Capitalize	131
20.	Adapt and Advance	137
21.	Amplify Your Strengths	141
22.	Review and Recalibrate	147
23.	Trust Your Instincts	151
24.	Wield Strategic Silence	155
25.	Focus on the Endgame	159
26.	Fortify Your Resolve	163
27.	Persist and Persevere	167
28.	Protect Your Energy	171
29.	Rest and Restore	175

A Carefully Crafted Tactical Guide: Grounded in Experience, Designed for Action

This Tactical Guide is more than a collection of strategies. This is a blueprint for navigating high-stakes moments, built from lived experiences and lessons forged in fire. Each strategy is a reflection of resilience: the times I've stood firm, the moments I've stumbled and learned, and the victories that came from reclaiming my power. These are not abstract ideas but practical tools, sharpened by experience and offered to you as a source of strength and clarity.

Every word is intentional, crafted to equip you with the insights and strategies needed to face uncertainty with conviction and purpose. Some strategies will inspire bold action; others will guide you toward stillness in the midst of chaos. Together, they form a Tactical Guide that meets you where you are, offering a path forward no matter the challenge.

How to Navigate Your Tactical Guide

To ensure this Tactical Guide serves you in the heat of any moment, the strategies are organized into clear categories, each guided by the emotions you may experience. Whether you're feeling emboldened, hesitant, or determined, these categories are designed to help you quickly find what you need.

This structure is both practical and adaptable:

- It grounds you when uncertainty strikes.
- It provides clarity when emotions threaten to overwhelm.
- It helps you act decisively when timing is critical.

This intentional organization ensures that you don't just read this Tactical Guide, you use in real time, aligning your emotions with your actions.

#theartofstrategicresistance

Honoring Emotions: Fueling Resistance with Purpose

High-stakes moments call on the full range of human emotion, from anger and frustration to hope and empowerment. Resistance isn't fueled by just one feeling. It arises from a spectrum of emotions that demand both recognition and purpose.

In this Tactical Guide, you'll find strategies that honor both the fire of anger and the light of optimism. Difficult emotions like anger, hurt, or fear are given direction, transforming them into momentum. Likewise, positive emotions like joy, confidence, and clarity are amplified, enabling you to build and sustain your strength. This dual approach ensures that you have the tools to act from any emotional state, using it as a source of power rather than a stumbling block.

Introducing Strategic Categories and Emotional Guidance

To help you navigate this Guide with intention, we've organized the strategies into categories that align with specific emotional states and strategic needs. These categories mirror the natural progression of resistance, starting with grounding yourself, then moving to bold action, and finally conserving your energy for what lies ahead.

By understanding the interplay between your emotions and objectives, you can approach each strategy with clarity and focus. While these categories offer a thoughtful framework, remember: this is *Your* Tactical Guide. Use it in a way that resonates with your needs, adapting the strategies to fit your unique path and circumstances. This structure is designed to empower you to act with purpose, whether you're steadying yourself before engagement or reflecting on the path forward.

With these categories as your compass, you'll find that the Tactical Guide adapts to your needs, meeting you at every stage of your journey.

Let's dive in.

#builtlikeourancestors

Tactical Strategies

Grounding and Gaining Clarity

Purpose: To provide foundational clarity and grounding when you're feeling overwhelmed, disoriented, or in need of focus.

- **Strategies Included:** Devise Your Strategy, Stand Your Ground, Scout the Terrain, Position for Power, Speak with Purpose, Speak Truth to Power, Trust Your Instincts
- **When to Use:** Use these strategies when emotions like overwhelm or confusion arise. They help you pause, assess, and establish a solid foundation.
- **Key Emotions Aligned:** Overwhelm, Confusion, Vision, Purpose

Building Strength and Allies

Purpose: To strengthen support systems, expand your influence, and empower your position within any given space.

- **Strategies Included:** Develop Your Playbook, Command the Room, Rally Your Allies and Advocates, Organize, Mobilize, Engage, Engage the Disengaged, Amplify Your Strengths
- **When to Use:** Use these strategies in moments of isolation or helplessness, or when you need to reinforce your position with allies. When you're feeling empowered and confident, these strategies will help solidify your strength.
- **Key Emotions Aligned:** Isolation, Helplessness, Empowerment, Confidence, Vision

#theartofstrategicresistance

Taking Action with Conviction

Purpose: To empower bold, decisive actions in moments where resistance or disruption is required.

- **Strategies Included:** Exploit the Gap, Speak Truth to Power, Challenge with Conviction, Disrupt Expectations, Demand Accountability, Execute with Precision
- **When to Use:** For times of anger, frustration, or determination, when the focus is on channeling your emotions into direct, impactful actions that disrupt norms and demand accountability.
- **Key Emotions Aligned**: Anger, Frustration, Hope, Determination, Vision

Navigating and Evolving

Purpose: To remain flexible and forward-moving through change, growth, and unforeseen circumstances.

- **Strategies Included:** Ponder and Deliberate, Engage the Opposition, Leverage and Capitalize, Adapt and Advance, Review and Recalibrate, Focus on the Endgame
- **When to Use:** When driven by hope, determination, or a sense of purpose. These strategies are useful for navigating dynamic, evolving challenges or when curiosity compels you to explore new pathways.
- **Key Emotions Aligned:** Hope, Determination, Curiosity, Growth-Oriented

Protecting and Sustaining

Purpose: To fortify your resilience, maintain boundaries, and preserve your energy for the journey ahead.

- **Strategies Included:** *Execute with Precision, Wield Strategic Silence, Focus on the Endgame, Fortify Your Resolve, Persist and Persevere, Protect Your Energy, Rest and Restore*
- **When to Use:** *When you feel vulnerable, fatigued, or need a moment to recharge. These strategies are also ideal when joy or satisfaction propels you forward while honoring your well-being.*
- **Key Emotions Aligned:** *Vulnerability, Fatigue, Joy, Satisfaction, Resilience*

You've got the blueprint. Now it's time to make it your own. These categories provide a starting point, but this Tactical Guide isn't about following rules, though my son Jordan does call me a rule follower. For you, it's about creating a battle plan that fits your life and your fight. The strategies ahead are flexible, powerful tools that you can adapt to meet the moment. Let's discuss how to use them to operate with clarity, confidence, and conviction.

How to Use This Tactical Guide

Today, our battlegrounds aren't limited to conference rooms or formal arenas. We're engaging online, in our communities, and in spaces where our presence, words, and choices carry weight. Each strategy in this Tactical Guide is designed to address the realities of modern life, empowering you to move forward with purpose and clarity in any setting.

#theartofstrategicresistance

Think of this Tactical Guide as both a toolkit and a trusted ally, one to revisit as often as needed. Start by exploring the categories: Are you looking for clarity? Seeking allies? Ready to make bold moves? Use these groupings to align your emotions and objectives with the strategies that best fit the moment.

Each strategy includes:

- **Be In The Know Prompts:** Each section begins with prompts to help you ground yourself in purpose and clarity. These guide you toward a self-aware and strategic mindset, ensuring you're prepared to engage fully.
- **Clear Actions:** Tangible steps that bring each strategy to life. These actions are adaptable, seamlessly fitting into the diverse professional and personal spaces where you're called to engage.
- **Protective Strategies:** High-stakes moments demand resilience and the preservation of your energy. These strategies are designed to fortify your peace of mind and strength, keeping you ready for what lies ahead.

As you move through the Tactical Guide, trust that every strategy, every prompt, and every action is designed to meet you where you are, whether you're on a high or at a crossroads, celebrating a win or recovering from a loss.

This Tactical Guide is yours to adapt and own. Some strategies will resonate immediately, while others may reveal their power as specific challenges unfold. Revisit, reflect, and apply them as needed. When it feels like so much is out of your control, remember this: you always have choices, you always have power, and with the right strategy, you can always find a way forward.

#builtlikeourancestors

Strategy

1 DEVISE YOUR STRATEGY

Be In The Know Prompts:

- ❖ **Know Your Mission**
  Begin by asking yourself why you're engaging. Why does this battle matter to you? What values, goals, or outcomes make it worth fighting for?

- ❖ **Know the Endgame**
  Visualize your desired outcome. What's the ultimate impact you want to make? What do you want to achieve, and how will it shape the world around you? Keeping the endgame in mind anchors every move you make.

Strategic Focus

This is where every battle plan begins: with strategy. Without a clear plan, we risk becoming reactive, distracted, and vulnerable to whatever challenges arise. Devise Your Strategy means mapping out your moves with purpose, thinking ahead, and preparing yourself to step into high-stakes situations, equipped and grounded.

In today's landscape, where divisiveness and hostility are often the norm, strategy becomes our weapon against chaos. They want us to act on impulse, to be thrown off guard by every move they make. But we're not here to react. We're here to respond. This strategy is about creating a plan for engagement that aligns with who you are, what you stand for, and where you're going.

#builtlikeourancestors

Actions:

1. **Define Clear Objectives**

    ✓ Make your objectives specific, grounded in reality, and directly tied to your mission. For example, if a short-term objective is to speak up in your community, make it actionable: outline where, when, and how. A long-term goal might be building a platform or network that amplifies voices aligned with your cause.

    ✓ ***Reflect:** How do these objectives align with your core mission? Clarity in your objectives will fortify your resolve when challenges arise.*

2. **Identify Your Strengths and Resources**

    ✓ Inventory the resources you can leverage, your skills, allies, platform, knowledge. List your top strengths and consider how each one can be applied here. This is not about identifying gaps; it's about maximizing what you already bring to the table.

    ✓ ***Reflect:** Where might you need additional support? Recognizing these areas ensures you're prepared without overextending yourself.*

3. **Create Contingency Plans**

    ✓ Strategy includes flexibility. For each objective, map out potential roadblocks and outline alternate routes. What if resistance arises? What if a key ally falls through? Prepare backup options for the obstacles you might face.

#theartofstrategicresistance

✓ **Reflect:** *How do you handle setbacks? Building contingency plans prepares you for the unexpected and strengthens resilience, keeping you grounded even if the path shifts.*

Protective Strategies:

➤ **Digital Safety:** As you plan, consider potential risks to privacy, especially if your objectives include online engagement. Guard sensitive information and use discretion when sharing. Familiarize yourself with privacy settings and keep personal details secure.

➤ **Mental Grounding:** Strategy is strengthened by a clear, grounded mind. Develop rituals to center yourself, whether it's taking a deep breath before engaging, pausing briefly before posting online, or grounding yourself before responding to tension. Protecting your mental clarity ensures you can step into strategy with intention.

Strategy

2 PONDER AND DELIBERATE

Be In The Know Prompts:

- **Know the Game**
  Take a moment to fully understand the dynamics at play. Consider the intentions, motivations, and potential moves of those involved. Strategic awareness is the first step in making wise choices. When you know the game, you don't play into it blindly.

- **Know Your Role**
  Before acting, be clear on the position you want to hold in this scenario. Are you a quiet observer, an active influencer, or a decisive leader? Knowing your role will help determine whether it's best to move forward, pause, or adjust.

- **Know Your Limits**
  Reflect on your own boundaries, resources, and energy. Strategic thinking includes recognizing when you are at your best and identifying conditions that may hold you back. By understanding your limits, you avoid overstretching and ensure you're acting from a place of strength.

Strategic Focus
The power of pondering and deliberating lies in its ability to provide insight before any action is taken. This strategy is about taking the time to slow down, gather information, and carefully consider your options before making a move. In the heat of decision-making, it's easy to fall into reactive choices, but Ponder and Deliberate encourages a reflective approach that allows you to see all angles. This strategy helps ground you, ensuring that any action you take is well thought out, deliberate, and aligned with your core mission.

#builtlikeourancestors

> Deliberation is a mark of strength and wisdom, not hesitation. It's the moment you grant yourself permission to pause and ensure that every move you make is intentional and precise, giving you the upper hand and conserving your energy for where it truly matters.

Actions:

1. **Gather and Analyze Information**

   ✓ Take time to gather the data, context, and perspectives relevant to the situation. By doing so, you create a more comprehensive understanding of what's at play and can identify any hidden risks or opportunities.

   ✓ *Reflect: What insights are you overlooking that could impact your next steps? What assumptions are you making that need to be re-evaluated?*

2. **Visualize Potential Outcomes**

   ✓ Mentally walk through the possible results of each action you might take. Consider both the best- and worst-case scenarios, thinking through the impact of each outcome on your overall mission.

   ✓ *Reflect: What are the likely consequences of each path? How can foreseeing potential outcomes shape your next move?*

#theartofstrategicresistance

3. Decide When and How to Move

- ✓ **Deliberate timing is key.** After weighing your options, choose not only what to do but precisely when to do it. A well-timed action is often more powerful than a quick reaction.

- ✓ **Reflect:** *What factors will signal that it's time to act? How can you best prepare yourself to seize the right moment?*

Protective Strategies:

- ➤ **Cultivate Patience:** Impatience often leads to impulsive decisions. By cultivating patience, you maintain control, giving yourself the grace of time to make a thoughtful, informed choice.

- ➤ **Create Space for Reflection:** Deliberation requires room to breathe. Schedule intentional pauses or quiet moments throughout your day to think, reassess, and prepare mentally. Reflection keeps your mind agile and reduces the likelihood of burnout from constant decision-making.

Strategy

3 STAND YOUR GROUND

Be In The Know Prompts:

- **Know Your Value**
  Recognize what you bring to the table. Own your value, your perspective, and your voice. No one else has your unique combination of insights, experiences, and strengths, and these matter.

- **Know the Rules**
  Every space has its unspoken rules, whether in person, online, or in writing. Understanding these norms equips you to assert yourself effectively, with confidence and control.

- **Know Your Limits**
  Stay true to your beliefs but choose your battles wisely. Not every challenge is worth your resources.

> **Strategic Focus**
> Standing your ground means staying rooted in your values and beliefs, even under pressure to compromise, conform, or remain silent. It's not about being defensive or confrontational. Instead, it's about having clarity on your purpose, embracing who you are, and knowing what lines you won't cross.
>
> When you stand firm, you build a foundation of integrity and strength that cannot be easily shaken.
>
> In critical moments, understanding your value and applying your strategies gives you the confidence to speak, act, and engage with purpose. This is about defining your boundaries and making your presence known, without apology.

#builtlikeourancestors

Actions:

1. **Identify Core Beliefs and Non-Negotiables**

    ✓ Take the time to define the values that are central to who you are and non-negotiable in your life. Write these down as clear, actionable statements to keep them top of mind. For example: "I will stand for equity," or "I will speak out against injustice." These statements become your guiding strategies.

    ✓ *Reflect: What beliefs are you willing to defend? When you are clear about what you stand for, you'll be prepared to face challenges that test your resolve.*

2. **Set Boundaries and Standards**

    ✓ Establishing boundaries means protecting your time or energy and creating the environment where you can thrive and make a meaningful impact. Define your personal and professional limits and put them into writing. This might involve learning to say "no" or refusing to tolerate behavior that conflicts with your values.

    ✓ *Reflect: What boundaries will support your mission? By clearly defining and enforcing these limits, you create a space that empowers your values to flourish.*

3. **Embody Your Presence**

    ✓ Standing your ground means showing up in every space with intention and authenticity. Let your body language, tone, and communication style consistently reinforce your values. This could mean maintaining steady eye contact, adopting a

#theartofstrategicresistance

confident posture, or ensuring your written and spoken words reflect clarity and purpose.

✓ **Reflect:** *What kind of presence do you want to project in each situation? When you approach every interaction with purpose and alignment, others will notice and respect the strength behind your actions.*

Protective Strategies:

➢ **Mindful Communication:** In both spoken and written words, remember this: once something is said or shared, it cannot be taken back. Consider the potential consequences of your words carefully. If you decide to speak or act, be prepared to stand by your choices. Words have power. They shape perceptions, spark action, and influence outcomes. Use yours with care, intention, and purpose.

➢ **Strategic Retreat as a Strength:** Standing your ground is a powerful act, but there are moments when stepping back demonstrates even greater wisdom. A strategic retreat is not a surrender. It is a deliberate decision to prioritize your energy and focus on battles that truly matter. Step back when the risks or costs outweigh the benefits, ensuring you have the strength and clarity to re-engage when the time is right.

➢ **Emotional Protection:** Standing your ground requires emotional intelligence and resilience. Be mindful of how much energy you invest in defending your position. Protect your emotional well-being by setting boundaries and cultivating support systems that help you recharge. Having healthy outlets for stress ensures you can remain strong, focused, and effective without burning out.

#builtlikeourancestors

Strategy

4 SCOUT THE TERRAIN

Be In The Know Prompts:

- **Know the Game**
  Assess the environment carefully. Is this a space where openness is encouraged, or does it require a more guarded approach? Understanding the dynamics of your surroundings allows you to navigate with purpose and intention.

- **Know the Players**
  Identify the key individuals in the space. Who holds influence? Who supports your efforts? Who might present opposition? Recognizing these dynamics helps you anticipate interactions and tailor your approach to achieve your goals effectively.

Strategic Focus
Every successful strategist understands the importance of studying the landscape before making a move. Scouting the terrain means observing the environment, whether physical or digital, and identifying its opportunities and challenges.

This goes beyond pinpointing allies and adversaries. It's about understanding how to move strategically, where to focus your efforts, and how to uncover and leverage hidden advantages.

When you take the time to scout the terrain, you gain clarity and confidence, enabling you to act in alignment with the space you're navigating. Awareness and preparation are the foundations of effective strategy. With a keen sense of direction, you're poised to engage with purpose and precision.

Actions:

1. **Observe the Atmosphere and Rules of Engagement**

   ✓ Every space has its own atmosphere and unspoken rules. Whether you're in a meeting, joining an online discussion, or preparing for a negotiation, take time to observe these dynamics. Pay attention to the tone of the conversation, the level of openness, and any visible or subtle power dynamics at play.

   ✓ *Reflect: Is this a space that calls for caution or openness? Understanding the nature of the environment equips you to navigate it effectively and with purpose.*

2. **Identify Key Players and Influencers**

   ✓ Understanding who is in the room, and their roles, is essential for navigating any environment. Take stock of those who hold influence, those who might support you, and those who could present challenges. This knowledge allows you to approach each interaction with foresight and confidence, minimizing surprises.

   ✓ *Reflect: Who are your allies? Who wields power in this space? Recognizing these roles helps you strategize effectively and focus your energy where it matters most.*

3. **Spot Hidden Advantages**

   ✓ Scouting the terrain involves both identifying challenges and uncovering opportunities. Look for unexpected allies, untapped

#theartofstrategicresistance

resources, or overlooked details that could work in your favor. Sometimes, the quiet observer or a seemingly minor connection can turn out to be a powerful asset.

✓ **Reflect:** *What elements of this space can you use to your advantage? Developing a keen eye for hidden opportunities allows you to seize moments that others might overlook.*

Protective Strategies:

- **Maintain Flexibility:** Scouting provides a solid foundation, but the landscape can shift unexpectedly. Dynamics may change, new players may emerge, or unforeseen information might come to light. Staying flexible allows you to adapt quickly and effectively, ensuring you're not caught off guard by surprises. Flexibility isn't a compromise. It's a strategic strength.

- **Guard Against Assumptions:** Never assume you have the full picture of an environment or its players. People and spaces often hold hidden complexities, and overconfidence can lead to missteps. Approach every situation with a mindset of curiosity and openness. Stay observant, remain willing to learn, and let your insights grow organically. This vigilance keeps you grounded and prepared for the unexpected.

Strategy

5 EXPLOIT THE GAP

Be In The Know Prompts:

- **Know the Rules**
  Understanding the rules of the game often exposes gaps within them. What limitations or constraints define the space, and how can you navigate these to your advantage? Gaps often stem from assumptions, unchallenged norms, or oversight. Identifying these blind spots empowers you to move with precision and strategy.

- **Know the Terrain**
  Assess your environment with care, whether it's a competitive landscape, a community, or a workplace culture. Gaps frequently appear as unaddressed needs, underutilized resources, or overlooked individuals. Recognizing these elements allows you to tailor a strategy others might not anticipate, giving you a distinct edge.

> **Strategic Focus**
> Success often hinges on recognizing and leveraging the spaces others overlook. Whether in warfare, business, or advocacy, gaps exist everywhere, unmet needs, ignored details, and untapped opportunities. The key lies in identifying these openings and acting decisively.
>
> This strategy isn't about exploiting others in a negative sense. It's about turning blind spots into opportunities and transforming limitations into strengths. By learning to "exploit the gap," you shift your perspective to one of possibility, uncovering paths that drive your mission forward with purpose and impact.

#builtlikeourancestors

Actions:

1. Identify Unclaimed Territory

- ✓ Look for spaces others haven't addressed. Is there a missing voice, an unspoken need, or a flaw in the current approach? These gaps are opportunities waiting to be transformed into powerful pathways for action. Use your insights to shape a strategy that fills these voids and sets you apart.

- ✓ *Reflect: Where are the blind spots in your environment? What steps can you take to occupy these overlooked spaces effectively?*

2. Turn Weaknesses into Strengths

- ✓ What others see as weaknesses or limitations can become your greatest assets. Gaps often appear as flaws, but with the right perspective, they can be flipped into strengths. Your ability to reframe and repurpose perceived shortcomings will set you apart and give you an edge.

- ✓ *Reflect: How can perceived limitations become assets? What opportunities arise when you view weaknesses through a fresh lens?*

3. Expand in Small Increments

- ✓ Exploiting gaps doesn't always require bold, sweeping moves. Small, deliberate actions can gradually shift dynamics and secure meaningful gains over time. Focus on methodical

#theartofstrategicresistance

progress, building momentum and strength as you navigate unexplored areas.

✓ **Reflect:** *How can incremental progress in overlooked spaces build your influence? What small, strategic steps can you take to expand your reach without drawing unnecessary attention?*

Protective Strategies:

- **Stay Nimble and Responsive:** Gaps can close quickly once they're noticed by others. To stay ahead, remain flexible and ready to adjust your approach as circumstances evolve. Being the first to act gives you an advantage, but agility ensures you can maintain it.

- **Use Discretion:** Capitalizing on gaps may attract unexpected attention. Move strategically, balancing visibility with impact. Keep sensitive plans secure and under wraps until the right moment to execute them. Discretion ensures your actions remain effective and protected from unnecessary scrutiny.

Strategy

6 POSITION FOR POWER

Be In The Know Prompts:

- **Know Your Role**
  Are you entering this space as a leader, an advisor, a supporter, an advocate, or an observer? Understanding your role is essential for determining how to approach the situation with influence. Your role defines the level of impact you can make and the strategy you should employ.

- **Know Your Value**
  Embrace the unique perspective, knowledge, and skills you bring to the table. Recognize your value and how it positions you to create meaningful impact. When you know your value, you're empowered to contribute with confidence and purpose.

> ***Strategic Focus***
>
> In high-stakes moments, power is defined by authority, presence, clarity, and the ability to leverage the position you hold. Positioning yourself for power means strategically choosing when and where to engage to maximize your influence and ensure your voice is heard. This isn't about forceful control, but about setting yourself up for lasting impact.
>
> When you position yourself powerfully, you move with intention. You select your battles wisely, focusing your energy on areas where you can make the greatest difference. This strategy involves aligning your actions with the position you aspire to hold, whether in a physical meeting, an online forum, or any space where decisions are made.

Actions:

1. **Identify Your Sphere of Influence**

   ✓ Every space you enter has areas where your influence is most potent. Take the time to identify these spheres, whether within a specific team, on a particular project, or during a group discussion. Knowing where your impact is greatest allows you to focus your energy where it counts.

   ✓ *Reflect: Where do you naturally hold authority or offer unique insight? By concentrating on these areas, you step into a position of power with authenticity and purpose.*

2. **Choose Your Battles Wisely**

   ✓ Not every issue or situation warrants your involvement. Choosing your battles wisely means focusing on matters that align with your mission and values, rather than being drawn into every challenge that comes your way. Identify where your voice will have the greatest impact and where you can truly make a difference.

   ✓ *Reflect: Which issues deserve your time and energy? Knowing when to engage and when to step back ensures your strength is preserved for moments where you can create the most significant impact.*

3. **Leverage Strategic Allies**

   ✓ Positioning yourself for power often involves building and utilizing alliances. Identify those who share your goals or values

#theartofstrategicresistance

and who can support your mission. Whether in professional or digital spaces, allies amplify your reach, offering strength in numbers and a shared sense of purpose.

✓ *Reflect: Who are your natural allies and advocates, and how can you support each other? Collaborating with like-minded individuals strengthens your influence and reinforces your position.*

Protective Strategies:

- **Pace Your Engagement:** In high-stakes situations, pacing yourself is crucial. Achieving power involves knowing when to lean in and when to step back. By doing so, you conserve your energy and avoid being drained by matters that don't warrant your full attention.

- **Be Strategic with Visibility:** Positioning yourself for power isn't always about being in the spotlight. Often, influence is built more quietly, through careful actions and thoughtful words. Be strategic in determining where visibility amplifies your impact, and where a more subtle approach is more effective.

Strategy

7 DEVELOP YOUR PLAYBOOK

Be In The Know Prompts:

- ❖ **Know Your Mission**
  Define Your Purpose. Clearly articulate the purpose behind your playbook. What core outcomes are you striving for, and why do they matter? A mission-driven approach offers clarity and direction, rallying those who believe in your vision and are committed to supporting it.

- ❖ **Know the Players**
  Identify those who naturally align with your mission, as well as those who may require encouragement or education to come on board. Understanding where others stand allows you to craft strategies that maximize support while anticipating and addressing resistance.

Strategic Focus
Those who wield influence, whether in politics, corporations, or communities, often rely on a strategic "playbook." This playbook, Tactical Guide, isn't merely a document or singular initiative; it's a structured vision with clear goals, strategies, and a blueprint for implementation. Project 2025 serves as a prime example of how a well-defined playbook can mobilize and engage. Its true power lies in the buy-in it generates among supporters, transforming them into dedicated advocates.

This strategy emphasizes the importance of creating a playbook that not only defines your mission but also inspires others to actively champion it. With clear messaging, a shared purpose, and authentic alignment, you can build a network of advocates who amplify your vision and sustain its momentum.

#builtlikeourancestors

Actions:

1. **Set Goals with Shared Purpose**

   ✓ Establish Clear Goals. Define your goals, from short-term wins to long-term outcomes, and present them in ways that others can easily understand and connect with. When people feel personally invested in the purpose behind your goals, they are more likely to align and engage.

   ✓ *Reflect:* How can you frame your mission and goals to inspire others to feel a personal connection? What language or imagery resonates most with your audience?

2. **Create Buy-In and Build Alignment**

   ✓ You don't build buy-in by imposing beliefs. Creating buy involves inviting people to see themselves as part of the mission. Share stories, examples, and values that make the vision relatable. By helping others find their role within the playbook, you transform passive supporters into active champions who amplify the message and bring others on board.

   ✓ *Reflect:* How can you create a sense of ownership in others, so they feel genuinely invested? What messages or values can you communicate to foster loyalty without manipulation?

3. **Craft Repeatable Messaging**

   ✓ Clear, memorable messaging turns a mission into a movement. Develop slogans, phrases, or talking points that are easy to remember and share. When your vision is expressed in simple,

#theartofstrategicresistance

relatable language, it spreads naturally, creating collective buy-in, even among those who may not fully grasp every detail.

✓ *Reflect: What language can you use to make your message memorable and easy to communicate? How can you empower others to become natural messengers of your vision?*

Protective Strategies:

- **Practice Transparency and Integrity:** Authentic buy-in is built on honesty and trust. Share your mission with integrity by clearly communicating both the vision and the "why" behind it. Transparency fosters loyalty and sustains trust over time.

- **Distinguish Buy-In from Indoctrination:** Indoctrination seeks rigid, unquestioning allegiance, often at the expense of personal connection and understanding. True buy-in respects individuals' agency, inviting them to align with the vision thoughtfully. Encourage questions, adapt where necessary, and honor the pace at which others choose to come on board.

Strategy

8 COMMAND THE ROOM

Be In The Know Prompts:

- ❖ **Know Your Role**
  Are you stepping in as a leader, an influencer, a collaborator, or a listener? Defining your role in advance ensures you enter the room with presence and intention, prepared to navigate the dynamics effectively.

- ❖ **Know the Endgame**
  What outcome are you aiming for in this engagement? Whether it's fostering agreement, inspiring action, or presenting an idea, having a clear vision of your goal will shape your approach and focus your energy.

Strategic Focus

Commanding the room is not about overpowering others, it's about stepping into spaces with confidence, clarity, and purpose. It's about owning your voice, valuing your contributions, and making an impact. This strategy is rooted in embodying the confidence that comes from understanding who you are and what you bring to the table.

Every room you enter, whether physical or virtual, is an opportunity to influence, connect, and lead. As you engage, remember my motto: "I belong everywhere I am, but I don't belong everywhere." This reflects the truth that while you have the right to occupy any space you enter, not every space is deserving of your presence.

Commanding the room isn't about conformity; it's about authenticity. It's an invitation to bring your unapologetic, authentic self into the room, grounded in your purpose and power. By discerning where your presence aligns with your mission and values, you amplify your impact without compromising who you are.

Actions:

1. **Cultivate Presence through Body Language, Tone, and Visuals**

    ✓ Presence is conveyed through body language, tone of voice, and visual impression. Maintain an upright posture, steady eye contact, and a tone that exudes confidence and assurance. Be deliberate in your appearance, what you wear and how you present visually should reinforce your purpose and align with your values. In virtual settings, pay attention to your background, lighting, and setup to create a professional and impactful visual presence.

    ✓ *Reflect:* What impression do you want to leave in this room? Embody the presence that reflects your values, and project your voice with intention and authority.

2. **Assert Your Voice with Clarity**

    ✓ Commanding the room means speaking with purpose and clarity. Avoid filler words, own your message, and embrace the power of pauses. Whether presenting, sharing an idea, or responding, ensure that your words are intentional and impactful.

    ✓ *Reflect:* Are your words aligned with your mission? When your voice is clear, purposeful, and confident, your contributions will resonate and draw attention.

#theartofstrategicresistance

3. Invite Engagement and Connection

✓ Commanding the room isn't just about asserting yourself; it's also about fostering engagement. Actively listen, invite input, and create space for dialogue, whether in a physical meeting or an online setting. Demonstrating respect for others' perspectives enhances your influence and builds connection.

✓ *Reflect: How can you foster connection in this room? Commanding the room is about creating shared purpose, not acting in isolation.*

Protective Strategies:

➤ **Guard Against Overextension:** While commanding the room is empowering, it can be draining if you're constantly in performance mode. Recognize when to step back and allow others to contribute, conserving your energy for pivotal moments.

➤ **Prepare for Misinterpretation:** In high-stakes interactions, especially online, your tone or intent may occasionally be misunderstood. Approach such situations with patience and respect, clarifying your message without compromising your authority.

Strategy

9 SPEAK WITH PURPOSE

Be In The Know Prompts:

- ❖ **Know Your Value**
  Understand the unique perspective your voice brings to any conversation. Speaking up begins with recognizing and embracing the significance of your insights and experiences. When you acknowledge your value, you speak with confidence and authority.

- ❖ **Know the Endgame**
  Before you speak, define your intention and objective. What is the purpose of your words? Whether it's to inspire, challenge, or advocate, clarity about your goal ensures that your message is impactful and aligned with your mission.

> **Strategic Focus**
> Speaking with purpose is about wielding your voice as a powerful tool for influence, truth, and change. In high-stakes moments, your voice can become a catalyst, challenging injustice, advocating for yourself or others, or introducing bold, innovative ideas.
>
> This strategy emphasizes recognizing the immense power of your voice and using it with intentionality. Speaking with purpose is not about adding to the noise; it's about making your words count. Thoughtfully chosen words, delivered with clarity and conviction, can inspire action, shift perspectives, hold others accountable, and align outcomes with your values and mission.
>
> To speak with purpose is to engage meaningfully, ensuring every word contributes to the change you aim to create. When you speak, you have the opportunity to lead, disrupt, and connect, all while remaining grounded in who you are and what you stand for.

#builtlikeourancestors

Actions:

1. **Identify What Needs to Be Said**

   ✓ Before speaking, clarify the essential message you want to convey. Whether advocating for a cause, addressing a concern, or presenting an idea, honing in on what's most important ensures your words have impact.

   ✓ *Reflect: What message will create the most value in this moment? Identifying your focus ensures your words are purposeful and directed.*

2. **Choose the Right Moment and Method**

   ✓ Purposeful communication requires mindfulness of timing and context. Consider when and how to share your message for maximum effectiveness, whether in a meeting, via written communication, or during a one-on-one conversation.

   ✓ *Reflect: Is this the right time and place to make your voice heard? Strategic timing and delivery amplify the impact of your words.*

3. **Speak with Conviction and Clarity**

   ✓ When it's time to speak, do so with confidence and precision. Minimize filler words, stay direct, and let your conviction shine through. Clear and confident communication ensures your message is heard and respected.

#theartofstrategicresistance

✓ **Reflect:** *Are your words expressing conviction? Is your message clear? Speaking with intention and confidence commands attention and ensures your voice resonates.*

Protective Strategies:

- **Stay True to Your Values:** Ground your words in your core beliefs. Avoid speaking impulsively or straying from your principles. Aligning your message with your values strengthens its authenticity and power.

- **Prepare for Resistance:** Recognize that speaking up may invite pushback. Anticipate challenges and be ready to reinforce your points calmly and confidently. Staying composed in the face of resistance ensures your voice remains strong and unwavering.

Strategy

10 RALLY YOUR ALLIES AND ADVOCATES

Be In The Know Prompts:

❖ **Know the Players**
Identify those who share your values and those whose support could amplify your voice. Allies and advocates come in many forms, from close confidants to influential supporters. Understanding who stands with you fortifies your impact and broadens your reach.

❖ **Know Your Mission**
Before seeking support, be crystal clear about your purpose. When you know what you're fighting for, you can inspire others with authenticity and confidence, creating genuine connections around your mission.

Strategic Focus
No warrior fights alone. Rallying allies and advocates is about building a network of support united by a shared purpose. Allies offer steady encouragement, while advocates go further, they actively champion your cause, pushing the mission forward. This strategy is about cultivating these relationships, nurturing mutual trust, and knowing when to rely on the collective strength of others to amplify your impact.

In high-stakes situations, surrounding yourself with people who believe in your vision elevates both your resilience and influence. Allies and advocates aren't merely supporters, they're partners in purpose. By uniting around shared values, you form a coalition that stands firm, ready to act, speak, and advocate as one. Together, your voices echo louder, your actions reach further, and your mission gains unstoppable momentum.

#builtlikeourancestors

Actions:

1. **Identify and Engage Your Allies**

   ✓ Begin by seeking out those who share your values and goals. These could be colleagues, mentors, or like-minded individuals within your industry or community. Reach out to establish genuine connections built on mutual respect and a shared purpose.

   ✓ *Reflect: Who aligns with your mission, and how can you engage them meaningfully? Building a network of allies requires intentional effort to foster trust and create a foundation of mutual support.*

2. **Elevate Advocates Within Your Network**

   ✓ Advocates go beyond support. They actively champion your mission. Identify these individuals in your circle and empower them to take on leadership roles. Their influence and commitment can significantly amplify your cause.

   ✓ *Reflect: Who has demonstrated dedication to your vision, and how can you encourage them to step into a more active role? Elevating advocates transforms supporters into partners, creating a stronger collective impact.*

3. **Foster Mutual Support**

   ✓ Building alliances is a two-way street. Find opportunities to reciprocate by supporting your allies' goals and missions. Whether it's amplifying each other's voices, sharing resources,

#theartofstrategicresistance

or offering valuable insights, creating reciprocal relationships fosters loyalty and a sense of shared purpose.

✓ **Reflect:** *How can you actively support your allies and advocates? Demonstrating commitment to their success strengthens your network and reinforces unity.*

Protective Strategies

- **Cultivate Boundaries:** Rallying allies and advocates doesn't mean saying yes to everyone. Be discerning about whom you invite into your circle. Surround yourself with individuals who align with your values, and don't hesitate to set boundaries with those who don't.

- **Prepare for Setbacks:** Even the strongest relationships can face challenges, such as miscommunications or disagreements. Approach these moments with openness and a willingness to work through issues thoughtfully. Maintaining trust and cohesion ensures long-term resilience in your network.

Strategy

11 ORGANIZE, MOBILIZE, ENGAGE

Be In The Know Prompts:

- ❖ **Know the Game**
  Gain a deep understanding of the landscape of power, influence, and resources in which you operate. Identify the key players who align with your mission and those who may pose challenges. Recognizing allies, potential supporters, and opposition equips you to anticipate needs and respond effectively.

- ❖ **Know the Players**
  Identify individuals in your network who are ready and willing to contribute to the mission. Determine who might need additional clarity about your purpose. Cultivating meaningful connections with like-minded individuals strengthens your collective power and amplifies your message.

- ❖ **Know Your Mission**
  A strong movement begins with a clear and focused mission. Define the core objectives of your organizing efforts and communicate them with clarity and conviction. When others understand and connect with your purpose, their commitment to the cause deepens.

- ❖ **Know Your Limits**
  Be honest about how much time, energy, and resources you can realistically commit to leading or participating in the cause. Recognizing your boundaries ensures sustainable involvement and avoids burnout.

> ***Strategic Focus***
> Real change often requires standing up individually and, more importantly, bringing people together. Organize, Mobilize, Engage is the strategy of aligning individuals around a shared mission and creating unstoppable momentum. Whether addressing a social issue, meeting a community need, or spearheading a workplace initiative, this approach focuses on building agenda-based communities, calling others to action, and establishing sustainable support networks.
>
> By organizing strategically, mobilizing efficiently, and engaging intentionally, you transform your vision into a movement that commands attention and drives meaningful change.

Actions:

1. **Build a Core Team**

   - ✓ Begin by identifying and gathering people who share your passion and are ready to actively contribute to your cause. Establish trust and a shared commitment within this core team, as they will be the foundation for organizing and spreading your mission.

   - ✓ ***Reflect:*** *Who in your network shares your values and mission? How can you cultivate an environment of trust and collaboration within this group?*

2. **Set Clear, Actionable Goals**

   - ✓ Break your mission down into achievable, specific objectives. Ensure each team member knows what they are working toward

#theartofstrategicresistance

and how their contributions support the larger mission. Setting clear benchmarks ensures progress and alignment.

- ✓ **Reflect:** *What specific goals can you set to create momentum in your mission? How can these goals empower each team member to take ownership of their role?*

3. **Create Community Connection Points**

    - ✓ Establish regular meetings, online forums, or events where members can connect, share updates, and offer support. Consistent communication builds trust, keeps everyone informed, and fosters a sense of belonging to a meaningful cause.

    - ✓ **Reflect:** *What channels of communication will best support your team's growth and connection? How will you ensure everyone feels heard and valued?*

4. **Engage the Broader Community**

    - ✓ Extend your reach beyond the core team by actively engaging others in your network. Host events, share content, or initiate collaborative efforts. Expanding the community fosters diverse perspectives, increases resources, and strengthens the movement's influence.

    - ✓ **Reflect:** *How can you engage others outside of your core team to build momentum? What messaging will resonate with a wider audience?*

#builtlikeourancestors

5. **Implement Accountability Practices**

    ✓ Set regular check-ins, progress reviews, and open discussions to ensure transparency and keep the team accountable to their roles and the mission. Accountability builds trust, encourages responsibility, and ensures everyone stays committed.

    ✓ *Reflect: How can you hold the team accountable in a supportive and inspiring way? What practices will help keep the mission on track?*

Protective Strategies:

➢ **Build Boundaries and Priorities:** Driving a movement can be demanding. Establish clear boundaries to safeguard your time and energy. Ensure your mission stays aligned with your core values, and maintain a clear, manageable focus for the group.

➢ **Foster a Culture of Support and Respect:** Create an environment where every member feels valued and respected. This not only builds loyalty but also nurtures the emotional resilience necessary for sustaining long-term efforts.

➢ **Stay Flexible but Focused:** As your mission expands, challenges will emerge that require adaptability. Stay open to refining your approach while remaining true to your core purpose. Flexibility ensures the movement evolves without compromising its foundational integrity.

#theartofstrategicresistance

Strategy

12 ENGAGE THE OPPOSITION

Be In The Know Prompts:

❖ **Know the Players**
Understand who you're engaging with. What are their values, motivations, and possible points of resistance? Recognizing their perspective enables you to anticipate their responses and frame your stance in ways that resonate effectively.

❖ **Know Your Role**
Be clear on your purpose in conversations with the opposition. Are you there to inform, challenge, or simply create an opening for future dialogue? Defining your role ensures that the interaction remains focused and constructive rather than confrontational.

> *Strategic Focus*
> Expand your reach by engaging thoughtfully with those who challenge your views. This isn't about convincing everyone or compromising your principles but about seeking opportunities for meaningful dialogue. Explore shared interests where they exist and identify allies who can bolster your cause while preserving the integrity of your mission.

Actions:

1. **Identify Potential Points of Connection**

    ✓ Begin by finding areas where even those on the opposing side may share a common value or concern. Highlighting these shared points can open the door to more productive dialogue.

#builtlikeourancestors

- ✓ **Reflect:** *What values or goals might overlap, even slightly? Pinpointing these can create a foundation for meaningful conversation.*

2. Ask, Listen, and Respond with Clarity

- ✓ Approach interactions with genuine curiosity and avoid making assumptions. Give them space to fully express their stance before presenting your perspective. By listening first, you increase the likelihood of being heard in return.

- ✓ **Reflect:** *How can you show that your engagement comes from a place of respect, even as you remain firm? Respect builds bridges, even over deep divides.*

3. Present Ideas as Exploration, Not Confrontation

- ✓ Frame your perspective in a way that invites consideration rather than opposition. Use thoughtful questions and insights to expand their viewpoint without making them feel challenged or cornered. The goal is to inform and gently shift perceptions.

- ✓ **Reflect:** *How can you introduce new ideas without triggering defensiveness? Often, small openings pave the way for gradual changes in perspective.*

Protective Strategies:

- ➤ **Establish Your Limits:** Recognize when a conversation has reached its limit. If the opposition becomes immovable or antagonistic, disengage respectfully and preserve your energy for more constructive efforts.

#theartofstrategicresistance

- **Stay Centered in Your Beliefs:** Engaging with opposition doesn't mean diluting your stance. Hold firmly to your values, using each interaction as an opportunity to clarify and reinforce them.

#builtlikeourancestors

Strategy

13 SPEAK TRUTH TO POWER

Be In The Know Prompts:

- **Know Your Mission**
  Be crystal clear about what you're advocating for, whether it's justice, opportunity, recognition, or change. Are you confronting harm or advancing a vision? This clarity sharpens your focus and strengthens your voice.

- **Know Your Value**
  Understand the power and importance of your voice. Speaking up doesn't demand perfection, just conviction. Your lived experience and expertise are more than enough to command attention and respect.

- **Know the Players**
  Assess your audience. Who has the authority to act on your message? Who might align with your goals, and who might resist? Knowing this helps you strategize effectively.

- **Know the Rules**
  Adapt your approach to the specific environment, whether it's a workplace, a family conversation, or a public platform. Understanding the context and its dynamics allows you to be both bold and strategic.

- **Know Your Role**
  Determine whether you're advocating for yourself, someone else, or a broader collective cause. Your role shapes how you position your message and how it resonates with others.

Strategic Focus

Speaking truth to power is about more than just challenging injustice, it's about affirming your values, advocating for your needs, and claiming your rightful space. This strategy invites you to wield your voice with intention, whether you're calling for accountability, demanding change, or standing up for what you deserve.

It's about rejecting silence as complicity and embracing your voice as a tool of empowerment and transformation. Whether you're pushing for equitable treatment at work, advocating for your community, or asserting your needs in business, this approach equips you to step into the moment with clarity and conviction.

Speaking truth to power is a balance, knowing when to disrupt and when to inspire, when to challenge and when to champion. It's a deliberate practice of aligning your voice with your values and advancing your mission boldly, unapologetically, and strategically.

Actions:

1. **Advocate for What You Deserve**

    ✓ Don't wait for someone else to recognize your value, advocate for yourself. Whether it's a promotion, opportunity, or recognition, speaking up ensures your contributions and value are acknowledged.

    ✓ **Reflect:** *What do you want or need, and how can you clearly articulate why it matters?*

#theartofstrategicresistance

2. Call Out Injustice or Harm

- ✓ Address harmful practices, statements, or behaviors with courage and conviction. Your voice has the power to challenge the status quo and demand accountability.

- ✓ *Reflect: How can you confront harm in a way that directly addresses the issue while fostering accountability?*

3. Inspire and Rally Others

- ✓ Speaking truth to power is an individual action and also about mobilizing collective energy. Use your voice to inspire others, align on shared goals, and create momentum for change.

- ✓ *Reflect: What message can you deliver to galvanize others into joining or supporting your mission?*

4. Set the Standard Through Advocacy

- ✓ Advocacy is as much about action as it is about intention. Speak up not just in reaction to problems but to proactively shape the future you envision. Align your words with your values and use them to set a tone that others can follow.

- ✓ *Reflect: How does speaking up for what you believe inspire others and create a ripple effect for broader change?*

5. Leverage the Power of Story

- ✓ Personal and collective stories are powerful tools for advocacy. They humanize issues and connect with audiences on an emotional level, making your message more relatable and impactful.

✓ **Reflect:** *What story or example can you share that aligns with your mission and reinforces your message?*

Protective Strategies:

➢ **Ground Yourself in Facts:** When advocating or challenging, back your position with facts. This strengthens your credibility and makes your voice more difficult to dismiss.

➢ **Practice Reframing:** Anticipate resistance and reframe the conversation when needed. Keep the focus on your purpose and goals rather than getting sidetracked by defensiveness or distractions.

➢ **Enlist Allies:** You don't have to advocate alone. Seek out allies who share your vision or values, and work together to amplify your message.

➢ **Prepare for Pushback:** Not every moment will lead to immediate change, and that's okay. Anticipate challenges and remind yourself that progress is a journey, not a single moment. Speaking up is about paving the way for meaningful transformation over time.

#theartofstrategicresistance

Strategy

14
ENGAGE THE DISENGAGED

Be In The Know Prompts:

- ❖ **Know the Players**
  Understand who around you is disengaged and why. Are they feeling overlooked, uninspired, or uncertain about their role? Identifying the root cause of their disengagement enables you to tailor your approach effectively.

- ❖ **Know Your Mission**
  Remember that engaging the disengaged serves a greater purpose. By reaching those on the sidelines, you strengthen the foundation of your mission. Building a coalition that amplifies previously unheard voices fosters inclusivity and collective progress.

> ***Strategic Focus***
> Disengagement doesn't always stem from disagreement. It can result from disillusionment, fatigue, or a sense of powerlessness. Successfully engaging the disengaged means drawing them into the cause, helping them reconnect, and demonstrating that their voice and participation are essential to the group's collective strength.

Actions:

1. **Create Safe Spaces for Expression**

   - ✓ Foster an environment where individuals feel safe to share their thoughts and concerns without fear of judgment or retribution. Sometimes, simply listening to their reasons for disengagement can open the door to deeper understanding and connection.

#builtlikeourancestors

✓ **Reflect:** *What might be holding them back from participating? Listening with empathy and without judgment can be the first step toward reigniting their interest.*

2. **Highlight Their Value and Influence**

   ✓ Remind disengaged individuals of the unique value and perspective they bring. Many people disengage because they don't see the impact of their contributions. Show them how their involvement strengthens the mission and enriches the overall effort.

   ✓ **Reflect:** *How can you clearly convey their potential impact? When people feel seen, valued, and appreciated, they're much more likely to re-engage with purpose.*

3. **Start Small to Build Connection**

   ✓ Re-engagement is often a gradual process. Begin with small, manageable actions or requests that help rebuild trust and confidence. As individuals start to see the positive effects of their involvement, their commitment will naturally grow.

   ✓ **Reflect:** *What small, meaningful steps can help them reconnect? Gradual engagement fosters confidence and renews their sense of purpose.*

Protective Strategies:

➢ **Pace the Process:** Re-engaging the disengaged requires patience. Be prepared for setbacks and avoid expecting

#theartofstrategicresistance

immediate results. A steady, thoughtful approach ensures sustainable progress.

- **Set Healthy Boundaries:** While supporting others, protect your own energy and resilience. Avoid letting their doubts or negativity derail your momentum. Stay focused and grounded as you encourage their journey toward re-engagement.

Strategy

15 CHALLENGE WITH CONVICTION

Be In The Know Prompts:

- **Know the Game**
  Recognize that there are often underlying motivations at play. Those in power may attempt to shut down your challenge by questioning your motives or strategies. Understand the dynamics and the tactics they might use, so you can sidestep their maneuvers and continue to press forward with purpose.

- **Know the Rules**
  When challenging decisions or outcomes, a clear understanding of the structure and rules governing the situation gives you a significant advantage. Knowing how things are supposed to work allows you to identify discrepancies and empowers you to question confidently and effectively.

> **Strategic Focus**
> When something doesn't feel right, speak up. Refuse to settle for passive acceptance. Challenge with Conviction is about standing firm and rejecting intimidation designed to silence you or force your conformity.
>
> When others attempt to manipulate perception or use social pressure to discourage you from raising your voice, remember this: your perspective and your challenge are valid. Don't be swayed by their efforts to label you as contradictory, difficult, or hypocritical. Recognize these tactics for what they are, attempts to suppress your dissent.

> This strategy equips you to persist, ask the necessary questions, and demand the clarity and accountability that the situation requires. Stay focused, maintain your resolve, and let your conviction drive you forward.

Actions:

1. Demand Transparency

- ✓ Transparency is essential when challenging decisions or results. If something feels hidden, glossed over, or distorted, insist on the details. Request facts, data, and explanations, even if it makes others uncomfortable. Clarity is your right, and it should never be compromised.

- ✓ **Reflect:** *What information or transparency is missing? How can your demand for clarity shift the power dynamic in your favor?*

2. Refuse Passive Acceptance

- ✓ Don't let the fear of criticism or perception prevent you from questioning decisions or results that don't add up. Passive acceptance often serves as a tool to maintain control. Actively challenge the status quo, making it clear that your questioning is grounded in integrity and strategy, not conflict for its own sake.

- ✓ **Reflect:** *How can you assertively communicate that your challenge stems from a commitment to integrity, not mere disagreement?*

#theartofstrategicresistance

3. **Frame Your Challenge as Due Diligence**

   ✓ Position your questions and challenges as a matter of responsibility and due diligence. If accusations of hypocrisy arise, root your response in your commitment to truth and transparency. Remember, questioning is not defiance, it's accountability.

   ✓ *Reflect:* *How does framing your challenge as due diligence enhance your credibility? What strengths does this approach bring to your position?*

Protective Strategies:

➢ **Strengthen Your Inner Resolve:** Challenging powerful decisions or questioning established norms requires a solid foundation of self-assurance. Build your resolve by anchoring yourself in the core values that guide your actions. When others question your motives, remind yourself that integrity and truth are at the heart of your challenge. This inner clarity acts as your defense against criticism aimed at undermining your conviction.

➢ **Reassert Your Intent and Control the Narrative:** Expect others to attempt to twist your intentions. Stay proactive by clearly articulating the purpose behind your challenge. Outline your concerns and emphasize that your goal is accountability, not conflict. By reasserting your intent and steering the narrative, you can counter misrepresentation and strengthen your credibility.

➢ **Set Boundaries to Guard Your Well-Being:** Criticism can become personal, especially when challenging deeply entrenched systems or beliefs. Establish firm boundaries on the feedback you allow to influence you, prioritizing input that aligns with your mission. By protecting your mental and emotional well-being, you ensure the strength to remain resolute in the face of intense scrutiny.

#theartofstrategicresistance

Strategy

16
DISRUPT EXPECTATIONS

Be In The Know Prompts:

❖ **Know the Rules**
Understand the norms and expectations of the space you're entering. Familiarity with what's expected enables you to plan strategically, knowing when to follow the rules and when to deviate for maximum impact.

❖ **Know Your Role**
Determine how you want to show up: as a challenger, an innovator, or an unexpected voice. By fully embracing your role, you can turn surprise into a powerful strategic advantage, using it to shift dynamics in your favor.

> ***Strategic Focus: Disrupting Expectations***
> Disrupting expectations is about challenging the status quo and introducing a sense of unpredictability. This approach emphasizes originality and intentionality, moving in ways that others might not anticipate. When you disrupt expectations, you break complacency, compel others to take notice, and reset the conversation.
>
> This strategy isn't about chaos or provocation; it's about deliberate actions that challenge assumptions and create space for new ideas.
>
> In high-stakes moments, unspoken rules and expectations often dictate behavior. While following them may seem safe, it can also render you predictable. Disrupting expectations grants you the freedom to act with impact, catching others off guard and ensuring your voice is heard.

#builtlikeourancestors

By embracing the power of surprise, you not only advance your mission but also redefine the parameters of what's possible within the space you occupy.

Actions:

1. **Identify Areas for Innovation**

   ✓ Seek out areas where the standard approach feels outdated or ineffective. Where can you offer something fresh and impactful? Pinpointing these opportunities allows you to disrupt expectations in a way that adds value and sparks meaningful change.

   ✓ ***Reflect:** What norms or practices can you challenge? Innovation doesn't always have to be bold. It can be subtle yet transformative. By introducing something new, you invite others to see things from a fresh perspective.*

2. **Use the Element of Surprise**

   ✓ Effective disruption often hinges on timing and nuance. Surprise might mean sharing an unexpected perspective in a conversation or taking a bold step to redirect a project. Be intentional about when and where you introduce the unexpected to capture attention and shift the focus meaningfully.

   ✓ ***Reflect:** How can you incorporate surprise into your approach? Ensure that every surprising action or idea aligns with your mission and has a clear, strategic purpose.*

#theartofstrategicresistance

3. Challenge Assumptions Respectfully

- ✓ Disrupting expectations doesn't mean dismissing others. Instead, challenge assumptions thoughtfully by sharing new insights or posing questions that encourage deeper thinking. This approach fosters collaboration and reframes discussions without creating unnecessary resistance.

- ✓ *Reflect: How can you challenge assumptions in a way that remains respectful and aligned with your values? Thoughtful disruption can open doors to innovative solutions and broaden perspectives, encouraging growth for all involved.*

Protective Strategies:

- ➤ **Prepare for Pushback:** Disruption can make others uncomfortable, particularly if they are invested in maintaining the status quo. Anticipate resistance and be ready to reinforce your ideas with clarity, confidence, and patience.

- ➤ **Embrace Flexibility:** Disrupting norms requires adaptability. If an idea doesn't resonate or achieve the intended impact, be open to adjusting and refining your approach. Flexibility ensures that your disruption remains purposeful and avoids creating unnecessary friction.

Strategy

17
DEMAND ACCOUNTABILITY

Be In The Know Prompts:

❖ **Know the Rules**
Recognize the standards and values that define your mission. Accountability begins with a shared understanding of expectations, providing a foundation for evaluating actions and decisions.

❖ **Know Your Role**
Are you stepping in as a leader, a peer, or an observer? Clarifying your role allows you to determine the most effective way to approach accountability, ensuring that your efforts align with your position and influence.

> *Strategic Focus: Demanding Accountability*
> Demanding accountability is about establishing and upholding a standard of responsibility for yourself and those around you. This strategy involves holding others to the values and commitments they have made, whether in personal relationships, professional environments, or broader initiatives.
>
> Accountability isn't about exerting control; it's about fostering integrity, ensuring alignment with shared goals, and creating an environment where everyone's contributions advance the collective mission.
>
> In high-stakes moments, accountability reveals who is truly committed and who may be falling short. By insisting on accountability, you reinforce a culture of honesty, shared purpose, and mutual respect. This clarity demonstrates that actions matter, and that integrity is not negotiable.

#builtlikeourancestors

> When approached with clarity and respect, accountability becomes a tool for building trust, supporting progress, and strengthening collaboration within any group or initiative.

Actions:

1. **Set Clear Expectations Early**

   ✓ Accountability begins with clarity. Whether in professional collaborations, partnerships, or shared projects, establish expectations from the start. Ensure everyone understands the values, goals, and standards you're striving for.

   ✓ *Reflect: What expectations need to be communicated upfront? Setting clear expectations early makes accountability a foundational standard rather than an afterthought.*

2. **Hold People to Their Commitments**

   ✓ When someone falls short or fails to meet agreed-upon standards, address the issue directly but respectfully. Focus on the actions and their impact, avoiding personal judgments. These conversations strengthen trust and reinforce accountability.

   ✓ *Reflect: How can you approach these discussions constructively? Addressing issues directly promotes responsibility while maintaining respect and openness.*

3. Model Accountability Yourself

- ✓ Mutual accountability is the most effective kind. Hold yourself to the same standards you expect from others and remain open to feedback. By exemplifying accountability in your actions, you inspire others to follow suit, fostering a culture of integrity.

- ✓ *Reflect: How can you model accountability in your behavior? Demonstrating integrity encourages others to see accountability as a shared value rather than an imposed rule.*

Protective Strategies:

- ➤ **Balance Accountability with Empathy:** Accountability doesn't mean rigidity. Pair it with empathy and compassion, understanding that people may face challenges. Approach situations with flexibility while remaining firm on core standards.

- ➤ **Avoid Over-Correction:** While demanding accountability is vital, overcorrecting can lead to defensiveness or resentment. Focus on the bigger picture, core values and commitments, and avoid micromanaging minor issues. This approach ensures a culture of respect and trust in both relationships and the broader mission.

#builtlikeourancestors

Strategy

18
EXECUTE WITH PRECISION

Be In The Know Prompts:

- ❖ **Know the Endgame**
  Before taking action, ensure your efforts align with your ultimate goal. Precision demands clarity, so keep your end goal at the forefront of your decisions.

- ❖ **Know Your Mission**
  Every action you take should serve your greater purpose. Executing with precision means that each step is intentional and directed toward achieving a clear objective.

- ❖ **Know Your Limits**
  Align your actions with your strengths and resources. Precision requires focus, so avoid overextending yourself. Instead, prioritize impactful moves that make a meaningful difference.

> ***Strategic Focus: Executing with Precision***
> Executing with precision is about making deliberate, impactful moves. This strategy emphasizes careful planning, unwavering focus, and a commitment to quality over quantity. In high-stakes situations, precision is the key to transforming effort into results. It's the difference between making a point and leaving a lasting impact.
>
> Precision doesn't equate to overthinking or hesitation. It's about purposeful action and clarity in the messages you send. Whether it's a word, a response, or a decision, every move should bring you closer to your mission. By committing to precision, you ensure that your actions reflect your values and contribute meaningfully to your goals.

#builtlikeourancestors

Actions:

1. **Focus on High-Impact Actions**

   ✓ Review your goals and identify the actions most likely to drive meaningful progress. Prioritize quality over quantity, selecting moves that create lasting impact rather than fleeting results.

   ✓ *Reflect: Which actions will have the most significant and meaningful effect on your mission? By focusing on high-impact, high-return efforts, you conserve energy while maximizing effectiveness.*

2. **Plan and Time Your Actions Thoughtfully**

   ✓ Precision relies on timing. Evaluate when to act, speak, or hold back. Whether it's waiting for the opportune moment in a conversation or choosing the perfect time to share a message, timing can be as critical as the action itself.

   ✓ *Reflect: Is now the right moment to make this move? Thoughtful timing ensures your actions have the maximum intended effect.*

3. **Communicate Clearly and Concisely**

   ✓ In high-stakes situations, clear communication is non-negotiable. Use precise language, avoid unnecessary fillers, and get straight to the point. A clear message eliminates ambiguity and ensures your words resonate.

#theartofstrategicresistance

✓ **Reflect:** *Is your message as clear and direct as it could be? Strong clarity reinforces the impact of your communication.*

Protective Strategies

- **Guard Against Overextension:** Precision involves understanding when not to act. Be mindful of your limits and avoid taking on too much at once. Staying focused requires boundaries, and precision thrives on intentionality.

- **Check for Consistency:** Regularly ensure your actions and words align with your mission and values. Consistency maintains credibility and reinforces your purpose, fostering trust and cohesion in your efforts.

Strategy

19 LEVERAGE AND CAPITALIZE

Be In The Know Prompts

- ❖ **Know Your Value**
  Acknowledge the unique leverage you bring to the table. It's not just about what you do; it's about how your insight, influence, and perspective can turn challenges into opportunities. Understanding your worth empowers you to command space, secure resources, and earn respect in ways that propel your mission forward.

- ❖ **Know the Game**
  Understand the dynamics and hidden opportunities within challenges. Recognize how these moments can shift power and open space for strategic action.

- ❖ **Know the Players**
  Identify the key figures in the moment, their motivations, and their influence. This awareness enables you to anticipate their moves and leverage their roles to your advantage.

- ❖ **Know the Rules**
  Understand both the explicit and unspoken norms governing the situation. Whether you operate within or beyond these rules, doing so strategically helps you position yourself effectively.

- ❖ **Know Your Endgame**
  What's your ultimate goal? Leverage requires direction. Knowing your "why" ensures that your actions contribute to something purposeful and lasting. A clear vision sharpens your response and amplifies your ability to capitalize on opportunities.

> ***Strategic Focus***
>
> Leverage and Capitalize invites you to see challenges, frustrations, and even performative gestures as moments rich with strategic potential. It's easy to feel disrespected or dismissed in these instances, but what if these very moments could become your greatest leverage? This strategy isn't about passively accepting indignities or suppressing your emotions. Rather, it's about embracing your feelings as fuel, channeling them into deliberate actions that build power, influence, or resources.
>
> This approach isn't about reacting impulsively. It's about owning the moment, shifting the narrative, and using every misstep, every hollow gesture, and every instance of resistance to your advantage. Even when others falter, you can create outcomes that strengthen your position and advance your mission.

Actions

1. Honor Your Emotions as Data and Power

- ✓ Fully acknowledge your feelings, anger, frustration, disappointment. These emotions are not only valid but also informative. Instead of reacting immediately, take a pause to ask, "What does this moment reveal? What advantage or leverage does it offer?"

- ✓ **Reflect:** *How can your feelings guide you toward a strategic response? What opportunity lies within the frustration?*

#theartofstrategicresistance

2. **Evaluate the Terrain for Leverage**

    ✓ Assess the situation strategically. Is there a way to redirect the energy of this moment, be it outrage, attention, or resources, into something that furthers your mission? Leverage is about recognizing when and how the dynamics of the moment align with your goals and using that to your advantage.

    ✓ *Reflect: What opportunities exist in the opposition or challenge before you? How can you position yourself to turn this situation in your favor?*

3. **Capitalize with Purpose and Precision**

    ✓ Transform reactive moments into lasting impact. Whether you're building momentum for a cause, responsibly monetizing a trend, or amplifying your voice to gain allies, seek ways to extend the reach of the moment beyond the immediate. Choose actions that resonate with your values and maximize the opportunity's impact.

    ✓ *Reflect: How can this moment be leveraged for sustained influence, resources, or visibility? What steps will ensure your actions align with both short-term and long-term goals?*

Protective Strategies:

➢ **Guard Your Integrity:** Balancing emotion and strategy require clarity. Ensure your actions reflect your values as you capitalize on the moment, maintaining authenticity and alignment with your purpose.

#builtlikeourancestors

- **Anchor in Purposeful Transparency:** If your response involves gaining resources or attention, communicate your purpose clearly. Show your audience that every action and every gain contributes directly to meaningful change.

- **Hold Space for Nuance:** Not every moment demands immediate action. Discern which opportunities are worth pursuing and which can be observed without intervention. This preserves your energy and ensures that every move you make is purposeful.

#theartofstrategicresistance

Strategy

20 ADAPT AND ADVANCE

Be In The Know Prompts:

❖ **Know the Game**
Recognize that circumstances change, and flexibility is essential. Understanding the landscape allows you to gauge when and how to adapt effectively.

❖ **Know Your Mission**
Stay focused on your mission. Even as you adjust to new challenges, find ways to stay aligned with your core purpose.

❖ **Know Your Limits**
Understand your boundaries as you adapt. Balance flexibility with your capacity and avoid overextending yourself.

Strategic Focus:

Adapt and Advance means cultivating the agility to shift your approach while continuing to move forward. In high-stakes moments, adaptability becomes a key advantage, enabling you to overcome setbacks and seize unexpected opportunities. This strategy is about responding proactively to change, staying resilient, and using flexibility as a tool for progress.

To advance, we must remain open to recalibration. Setbacks and surprises are inevitable, but they don't have to derail you. By adapting to the situation at hand, you strengthen your path forward, transforming obstacles into stepping-stones toward your mission.

Actions:

1. **Stay Open to New Perspectives**

   ✓ Adapting requires openness to fresh viewpoints and alternative approaches. When faced with a challenge, consider perspectives you may not have initially valued or methods you haven't tried. This openness can reveal innovative solutions and unexpected paths forward.

   ✓ **Reflect:** *What new perspectives could help you overcome this challenge? Staying open-minded strengthens your adaptability, ensuring you remain flexible as you advance.*

2. **Reassess and Adjust Your Strategy**

   ✓ Adapting doesn't mean losing focus. Adapting means recalibrating to stay aligned with your end goals. When a challenge arises, pause to reassess your strategy. Minor adjustments, whether to timing, resources, or actions, can often pave the way for continued progress.

   ✓ **Reflect:** *How can you adjust your strategy to meet the current situation? Reassessing helps you realign with your mission and keep moving forward.*

3. **Embrace Resilience as a Key to Advancement**

   ✓ Moving forward in the face of obstacles requires resilience. View setbacks as part of the journey, not as defeats. Each time you adapt and advance, you strengthen your ability to navigate future challenges with agility and confidence.

   #theartofstrategicresistance

✓ **Reflect:** *How can this setback propel you forward? Building resilience ensures that, no matter the obstacle, you continue moving with purpose.*

Protective Strategies:

➤ **Limit Attachment to Original Plans:** Adaptability is about flexibility, so release any rigid attachments to how things "should" go. Embracing new routes and ideas keeps you from feeling discouraged when plans shift, allowing you to advance regardless of the path.

➤ **Anticipate Potential Obstacles:** Part of adapting to advance is anticipating where challenges might arise. While you can't predict everything, mentally preparing yourself for adjustments keeps you ready to pivot and persist, maintaining momentum even in uncertainty.

Strategy

21 AMPLIFY YOUR STRENGTHS

Be In The Know Prompts:

❖ **Know Your Role**
Understand how your unique strengths position you in any space. Are you the strategist, the visionary, the executor, or the connector? Knowing your role clarifies how your strengths contribute to the bigger picture, enabling you to make the most of your abilities.

❖ **Know the Game**
Recognize the dynamics of the space you're in and identify where your strengths give you an advantage. This awareness ensures your actions are intentional and strategic, not wasted, or misguided.

❖ **Know the Rules**
To amplify your strengths effectively, you must understand the expectations, boundaries, and opportunities within the environment. Knowing the rules allows you to use your strengths with precision and purpose, maximizing your impact.

Strategic Focus:
Amplifying your strengths is about identifying what you do best and turning it into a source of power, influence, and growth. In high-stakes moments, strengths are not static traits. They're dynamic tools you can use to shift outcomes, create opportunities, and leave a lasting impact.

This strategy challenges you to not only identify your strengths but to amplify them in ways that align with your goals and values.

#builtlikeourancestors

> Whether through influence, skill, or leadership, your strengths are the foundation for both personal and collective victories. Amplify Your Strengths is about using what makes you exceptional to create exceptional results.

Actions:

1. **Discover Your Strengths Through Reflection and Feedback**

    ✓ Begin by asking yourself key questions: What do others consistently praise you for? What feels effortless to you but impactful to others? What challenges have you overcome using your unique skills?

    ✓ Seek feedback from trusted colleagues, friends, or mentors. Sometimes, our most powerful strengths are the ones we take for granted.

    ✓ *Reflect: What strengths emerge as themes across your experiences? How do they align with your current goals?*

2. **Create a Strengths Map**

    ✓ List your strengths and categorize them: technical skills, interpersonal abilities, leadership qualities, or visionary thinking. For each, note examples of how you've used them successfully in the past.

    ✓ Identify areas where you can use these strengths more intentionally. Consider how they align with your mission and how they can be leveraged in high-stakes moments.

#theartofstrategicresistance

- ✓ **Reflect:** *How can this map guide you toward opportunities where your strengths are most impactful?*

3. Showcase Strengths with Purpose

- ✓ Strengths gain power when they're visible. Whether through public speaking, strategic conversations, or thought leadership, use opportunities to showcase your strengths. This isn't about arrogance; it's about intentional visibility.

- ✓ **Reflect:** *What platforms, spaces, or relationships allow you to demonstrate your strengths authentically and effectively?*

4. Strategically Develop and Expand Your Strengths

- ✓ Amplification includes growth. Identify ways to stretch your strengths beyond current limits, whether through learning, collaboration, or stepping into roles that challenge you. Growth within strengths builds resilience and influence.

- ✓ **Reflect:** *What steps can you take to evolve your strengths into new areas of impact or leadership?*

Protective Strategies:

- ➢ **Guard Against Overconfidence:** Amplifying your strengths is vital, but staying grounded ensures you remain adaptable and open to growth. Overconfidence can close doors to opportunities for collaboration and feedback.

- ➢ **Balance Strength with Respect and Grace:** Using your strengths effectively means acknowledging the contributions of others and fostering a spirit of mutual support. Respect and grace allow your strengths to uplift and inspire rather than overwhelm.

➤ **Avoid Misusing Your Strengths:** Even the most powerful strengths can become liabilities if used recklessly or without intention. Always align your actions with your values and the greater mission to ensure your strengths serve a meaningful purpose.

➤ **Stay Open to Growth:** Don't just stick to what you already know or are good at. Be open to evolving. Recognize when a strength needs sharpening or when it's time to develop something new.

Strategy

22 REVIEW AND RECALIBRATE

Be In The Know Prompts:

- **Know Your Mission**
  Reflect on how your recent actions align with your mission. This ensures you're progressing in the right direction and staying true to your purpose.

- **Know the Endgame**
  Revisit your ultimate goal and assess whether any adjustments are needed. Regular reflection helps you keep your eye on the prize, adapting, as necessary.

Strategic Focus:
In any high-stakes journey, regular reflection is essential for staying aligned and effective. Reviewing and recalibrating involves taking a step back to evaluate what's working, what isn't, and how you might adjust your approach. This strategy is about continuous learning and refinement, recognizing that no strategy is perfect, and that growth comes from adaptation and insight.

Reflection strengthens your resilience by allowing you to learn from both successes and setbacks. It's a powerful tool for growth, helping you refine your strategies and sharpen your focus. By making reflection an active part of your process, you remain flexible, grounded, and ready for whatever comes next.

#builtlikeourancestors

Actions:

1. **Assess Your Recent Actions and Outcomes**

   ✓ Take time to evaluate your recent actions. Consider what went well, what you would change, and what you've learned. An honest assessment allows you to gain valuable insights and refine your approach moving forward.

   ✓ **Reflect:** *What have recent experiences taught you? Reviewing your actions provides clarity and informs future decisions.*

2. **Identify Areas for Adjustment or Growth**

   ✓ Use reflection as an opportunity to recalibrate. Identify any areas where a shift could strengthen your mission, whether it's adjusting your approach, developing a skill, or building on a strength.

   ✓ **Reflect:** *Where can you improve or adjust? Regular recalibration ensures your approach stays relevant and aligned with your mission.*

3. **Celebrate Progress and Refocus**

   ✓ Reflection isn't just about improvement; it's also about celebrating your wins. Acknowledge the progress you've made and the challenges you've overcome. Recognizing success reinforces your commitment and energizes you for what's next.

   ✓ **Reflect:** *What progress are you proud of? Celebrating progress renews your motivation and keeps your focus sharp.*

#theartofstrategicresistance

Protective Strategies:

- ➢ **Avoid Perfectionism:** Reflection can sometimes lead to over analysis. Be kind to yourself. Focus on learning, not perfection. Constructive reflection builds resilience without adding unnecessary pressure.

- ➢ **Create a Reflection Routine:** Schedule regular times for reflection, whether weekly, monthly, or after key milestones. This habit keeps you grounded and fosters consistent growth and recalibration.

Strategy

23 TRUST YOUR INSTINCTS

Be In The Know Prompts:

- ❖ **Know Your Role**
  Understanding your role helps you tune into your intuition and make choices that align with your mission. Trusting your instincts begins with clarity on how you're meant to show up.

- ❖ **Know the Game**
  Familiarity with the rules and dynamics of the space allows you to blend logic with intuition, making decisions that feel right and serve your purpose.

- ❖ **Know Your Limits**
  Self-awareness and discernment help you identify challenges worth pursuing and recognize those that may compromise your well-being.

Strategic Focus:
Trusting your instincts means listening to your inner voice and embracing your natural sense of direction. While logic and strategy are essential, intuition can guide you when answers aren't clear or when decisions need to be made swiftly. This strategy is about blending insight with instinct, recognizing that sometimes your best guide lies within.

Developing trust in your instincts is especially important in high-stakes moments, where time is limited, or logic alone may not provide clarity. By tuning into your intuition, you cultivate a personal compass that allows you to navigate uncertainty with confidence and ease.

Actions:

1. Tune Into Your Inner Voice

- ✓ Begin developing intuition by practicing self-awareness. In moments of doubt or challenge, listen to your gut response. Often, your instincts reflect a combination of experience, values, and subconscious awareness.

- ✓ *Reflect: What is your inner voice telling you right now? Tuning into this guidance allows you to integrate instinct with strategic thinking.*

2. Use Instinct to Complement Strategy

- ✓ Balance intuition with logic. Trust your gut when it aligns with the information you've gathered, allowing instinct to guide you when logic alone isn't enough. Intuition can provide unique insights or nudge you toward options you might not have considered.

- ✓ *Reflect: How does your intuition align with the information at hand? Combining intuition with strategy strengthens your decision-making.*

3. Practice Confidence in Your Instincts

- ✓ The more you trust your instincts, the stronger they become. When you make decisions based on intuition, embrace them with confidence. Practice taking small actions that reflect your instinct, building trust in your inner guidance over time.

#theartofstrategicresistance

✓ **Reflect:** *What decisions can you make based on instinct today? Practicing this trust creates a reliable inner compass that empowers you in high-stakes moments.*

Protective Strategies:

- **Distinguish Between Fear and Intuition:** Sometimes, fear or self-doubt can mask itself as intuition. Practice recognizing the difference. True intuition tends to feel clear and grounded, while fear often feels heavy or urgent.

- **Balance Intuition with Objectivity:** While trusting your instincts is valuable, it's essential to remain open to facts and new information. Allow intuition to guide you, but let objectivity balance your approach for a well-rounded perspective.

#builtlikeourancestors

Strategy

24 WIELD STRATEGIC SILENCE

Be In The Know Prompts:

- ❖ **Know the Rules**
  Silence is powerful, but it's essential to understand when and where it has the most impact. Assess the dynamics of the space to determine when silence will serve you best.

- ❖ **Know Your Role**
  Decide if your role in this moment is to observe, absorb, or act. Strategic silence can hold as much power as speaking. Knowing your role helps you determine the right approach.

> ### Strategic Focus:
> In high-stakes communication, silence is often as impactful as words. Wielding strategic silence means choosing when to hold back, when to pause, and when to let silence speak for itself. Silence can create space for reflection, maintain control in a conversation, or allow others to reveal more than they intended. It is a subtle yet powerful tool, one that requires discernment and intention.
>
> This is not about withholding or retreating. Strategic silence is about understanding that, sometimes, the most powerful statement you can make is through restraint. This strategy encourages you to harness silence to amplify your presence, create room for observation, and influence outcomes.

Actions:

1. Pause Before Responding

- ✓ In moments of pressure, pausing helps you gather your thoughts and conveys confidence. A well-timed pause gives others space to consider your words and often prompts them to fill the silence, revealing their thoughts or intentions.

- ✓ *Reflect: How can a pause shift the dynamic of this conversation? Pausing before responding signals confidence and gives you the opportunity to guide the flow of the exchange.*

2. Hold Space for Listening and Observation

- ✓ Silence can create space for active listening and deeper understanding. Use silence to observe both verbal and nonverbal cues, noticing what's left unsaid. This can provide insight into the other person's perspective or uncover underlying dynamics.

- ✓ *Reflect: What can you learn by observing without an immediate response? Silence allows you to gather information and gain clarity before deciding on your next move.*

3. Use Silence as a Response

- ✓ Sometimes, saying nothing speaks volumes. In situations where you want to convey disapproval, discomfort, or the need for reflection, silence can be a powerful response. It forces others to sit with their words, often prompting self-reflection or an unprompted shift in behavior.

#theartofstrategicresistance

✓ ***Reflect:*** *How can silence communicate your message without words? Using silence as a response can shift power dynamics, encouraging others to reconsider their actions or words more carefully.*

Protective Strategies:

➢ **Set Boundaries on Silence:** While silence is powerful, it should be used intentionally. Overusing silence may lead others to misinterpret your intentions. Use it selectively and purposefully to avoid diminishing its impact.

➢ **Prepare for Misunderstandings:** Strategic silence can be misread, especially in digital spaces. Be ready to clarify if necessary, ensuring that your silence isn't mistaken for disinterest or avoidance.

Strategy

25 FOCUS ON THE ENDGAME

Be In The Know Prompts:

- **Know the Endgame**
  What is your ultimate goal? Clearly defining your endgame provides a destination that anchors your decisions and actions with purpose. When you know where you're headed, it becomes easier to chart a meaningful course.

- **Know Your Mission**
  Ensure that every step you take aligns with your broader mission. Staying rooted in your mission helps you maintain consistency and direction, even in the face of complexity or uncertainty.

Strategic Focus
In high-stakes situations, clarity about the endgame is essential. As Stephen Covey famously said, "Start with the end in mind." Keeping your ultimate goal front and center ensures that each action, decision, and conversation propels you closer to that objective.

This strategy is about anchoring yourself to a clear purpose, creating a steady guidepost amidst distractions or challenges. By focusing on the endgame, you reduce the risk of being swayed by temporary setbacks or entangled in unnecessary conflicts. Instead, this mindset encourages you to approach every interaction with intentionality, using your endgame as your compass for decision-making and progress.

Actions:

1. **Define Your Desired Outcome**

   ✓ Take the time to clearly articulate what success looks like in this situation. Whether it's achieving agreement, building influence, or driving meaningful change, having a defined outcome gives you a tangible target to work toward.

   ✓ ***Reflect:*** *What does success look like for you in this context? Defining the outcome sharpens your focus, helping you visualize the endgame and direct your energy where it will have the greatest impact.*

2. **Align Actions with Your Endgame**

   ✓ Regularly ensure that your actions align with your ultimate goal. When making decisions, ask yourself whether they bring you closer to the desired outcome. Intentional alignment ensures that your efforts remain focused and purposeful.

   ✓ ***Reflect:*** *Are your actions moving you closer to your goal? Performing regular alignment checks helps you stay on track and avoid wasting time or energy on distractions.*

3. **Avoid Unnecessary Battles**

   ✓ Keeping your eye on the endgame also means recognizing when to disengage. Not every conflict or challenge deserves your energy. By prioritizing the bigger picture, you can conserve your resources for the battles that truly matter.

#theartofstrategicresistance

✓ **Reflect:** *Is this worth engaging in? Focusing on your endgame allows you to allocate your time and energy where they'll have the greatest impact.*

Protective Strategies:

- **Set Boundaries on Engagement:** Focusing on the endgame requires selective investment of your time and energy. Establish clear boundaries to prevent burnout and distractions, ensuring your efforts remain concentrated on actions that align with your mission.

- **Regularly Reevaluate the Goal:** As you progress, the endgame may evolve with new insights or changing circumstances. Reassess your goals periodically to ensure they remain aligned with your mission and the impact you aim to create. This adaptability allows you to stay purposeful, even as the path shifts.

Strategy

26 FORTIFY YOUR RESOLVE

Be In The Know Prompts:

- ❖ **Know Your Value**
  Recognize and embrace the unique perspective and strengths you bring to the table. Your value is the foundation of your confidence, helping you remain steadfast in moments of doubt or challenge.

- ❖ **Know Your Mission**
  Stay deeply connected to your mission. Understanding your "why" strengthens your commitment and provides clarity, even when the path becomes difficult. When you know what you're fighting for, it's easier to stand firm and move forward with purpose.

> *Strategic Focus*
> Fortifying your resolve means developing a mental and emotional foundation that can withstand pressure, setbacks, and uncertainty. In high-stakes situations, challenges may feel insurmountable, and doubt can creep in. This strategy emphasizes cultivating resilience and inner strength, ensuring that no matter what you encounter, you have the determination to keep moving forward.
>
> Resilience doesn't require ignoring difficulties or pushing forward blindly. Instead, it's about recommitting to your mission and values while nurturing your mental and emotional well-being. By reinforcing your foundation, you can face any situation with clarity, purpose, and unshakable resolve.

#builtlikeourancestors

Actions:

1. **Cultivate Inner Confidence**

   ✓ Building resolve begins with confidence in your abilities and dedication to your mission. Reflect on past successes, strengths, and moments of courage that remind you of your resilience. Trusting in your capacity to overcome challenges fortifies your inner strength and prepares you for what lies ahead.

   ✓ *Reflect: What past experiences remind you of your strength and perseverance? Recalling these moments reinforces your belief in yourself and your mission.*

2. **Develop Daily Practices for Resilience**

   ✓ Resilience isn't a single act. It's a consistent practice. Create daily habits that nurture your mental and emotional strength, such as meditation, journaling, physical activity, or quiet reflection. These routines provide the tools you need to face obstacles with a clear and steady mind.

   ✓ *Reflect: What daily practices help you feel grounded and resilient? Integrating these habits builds a solid foundation, even during challenging times.*

3. **Stay Connected to Your Support System**

   ✓ Resilience often grows through connection. Lean on a network of trusted allies, mentors, or friends who share your vision and encourage your progress. Having a support system reminds you

#theartofstrategicresistance

of your strength and helps you feel supported when challenges arise.

✓ **Reflect:** *Who are the people in your life who inspire and uplift you? Reaching out to them can provide perspective, encouragement, and a renewed sense of determination.*

Protective Strategies:

➢ **Guard Against Negativity:** Protect your mental and emotional space by limiting exposure to negative influences. Avoid environments or individuals that drain your energy or cause self-doubt. Surrounding yourself with positivity is essential to maintaining resilience.

➢ **Reaffirm Your Mission Regularly:** When your resolve feels tested, revisit your "why." Reconnect with the reasons you began your journey and the impact you're working toward. This clarity fuels your commitment and strengthens your focus, even during difficult moments.

Strategy

27

PERSIST AND PERSEVERE

Be In The Know Prompts:

❖ **Know Your Mission**
Clarify the long-term outcome you're working toward and how persistence supports this vision. Understanding your mission provides a sense of purpose, especially when the journey becomes challenging.

❖ **Know Your Value**
In moments of prolonged resistance, remember your intrinsic worth and the unique contributions you bring. Even when progress feels slow or invisible, your persistence has a lasting impact and carries undeniable influence.

❖ **Know Your Endgame**
Keep the ultimate goal in focus. Seeing beyond temporary obstacles helps you maintain perspective and reminds you why the journey is worth the effort. The endgame serves as your compass, guiding you through resistance with unwavering resolve.

Strategic Focus
Resistance is not a one-time effort; it's often a prolonged journey requiring endurance and intentionality. Persist and Persevere emphasizes staying the course when progress is incremental, opposition is strong, or support seems scarce.

Endurance becomes your most powerful tool, a steady, deliberate push forward despite challenges or setbacks. Yet, this principle isn't about blind perseverance. It's about a steadfast commitment that is:

#builtlikeourancestors

- Aligned with your vision,
- Anchored in purpose, and

Fueled by your resolve to overcome obstacles.

By keeping your mission, value, and endgame at the forefront, persistence transforms into a strategic act of resistance, bringing you closer to the impact you are determined to achieve.

Actions:

1. **Set Small, Achievable Milestones**

   - ✓ Break your larger goal into smaller, attainable steps to make progress more tangible and rewarding. Each small victory strengthens your resolve and provides the momentum to keep going. Celebrating these wins reminds you of how far you've come.

   - ✓ *Reflect: How can breaking this journey into smaller steps make it feel more manageable? What are three small wins you can aim for this week?*

2. **Strengthen Your Support Network**

   - ✓ Persisting through challenges can feel isolating, but a strong support network can be a vital source of encouragement and perspective. Surround yourself with people who remind you of your worth and share your vision.

#theartofstrategicresistance

✓ *Reflect: Who in your life offers strength and encouragement? How can you lean on their support when persistence feels difficult?*

3. Use Setbacks as Stepping Stones

✓ Obstacles are inevitable, but they don't define your journey. Instead, treat each setback as a learning opportunity. Every challenge faced builds resilience and sharpens your ability to navigate future hurdles.

✓ *Reflect: What has this challenge taught you? How can you use these lessons to guide your next steps?*

Protective Strategies:

➢ **Preserve Your Energy:** Identify and minimize what drains you. Endurance requires sustained energy, so prioritize self-care and rest to protect your well-being.

➢ **Anchor in Affirmations:** When persistence feels heavy, turn to affirmations that reaffirm your mission and remind you of your ability to persevere.

➢ **Embrace the Process:** Persistence isn't just about reaching the destination. It's a journey of growth. Every step forward builds your character, strengthens your resilience, and brings you closer to your goal.

#builtlikeourancestors

Strategy

28 PROTECT YOUR ENERGY

Be In The Know Prompts:

❖ **Know Your Value**
Understand the unique contributions you bring to every interaction. Honoring your value starts with recognizing that your energy is a precious resource, worthy of preservation and respect.

❖ **Know the Endgame**
Stay focused on what matters most in the long run. By aligning your energy with your highest priorities, you ensure that every effort contributes to your mission and serves your ultimate goals.

❖ **Know Your Limits**
Pay attention to your energy levels and recognize when it's time to step back. Respecting your limits allows you to protect your well-being and maintain resilience.

Strategic Focus
In high-stakes situations, energy is one of your most valuable resources. Protecting your energy means being intentional about how, when, and where you invest it. This is not about avoiding challenges or withdrawing from responsibilities; it's about acknowledging that your capacity isn't infinite. Strategic energy management ensures that you stay effective and aligned with your mission over the long term.

Preserving your energy involves setting boundaries, saying no when necessary, and prioritizing self-care. These practices allow you to make thoughtful, intentional choices that keep you grounded, focused, and ready for the challenges ahead.

#builtlikeourancestors

Actions:

1. **Set and Enforce Boundaries**

   ✓ Boundaries are essential for conserving your energy and maintaining balance. Clearly define what you're willing to engage with in both personal and professional spaces, and don't shy away from communicating these limits when necessary. If others challenge your boundaries, reinforce them with confidence and consistency.

   ✓ *Reflect: What boundaries are essential to protect your energy? Establishing and upholding these limits creates a secure space where you can recharge and focus on what truly matters.*

2. **Prioritize Self-Care and Rest**

   ✓ Your energy thrives when you prioritize your well-being. Dedicate time to practices that restore and nourish you, such as restful sleep, exercise, hobbies, or quiet reflection. Self-care isn't a luxury; it's a critical component of resilience and clarity.

   ✓ *Reflect: How can you make self-care a consistent part of your routine? Committing to rest and renewal enhances your ability to face challenges with strength and focus.*

3. **Invest in High-Impact Activities**

   ✓ Protecting your energy requires intentionality in how you spend it. Direct your efforts toward activities and projects that align with your mission and deliver meaningful outcomes. Release

#theartofstrategicresistance

tasks or obligations that drain you without significant value or return.

✓ **Reflect:** *Are your actions aligned with your core priorities? Focusing on high-impact efforts ensures your energy is spent purposefully and effectively.*

Protective Strategies:

➢ **Guard Against Burnout:** Overextending yourself can lead to burnout, often before you even realize it. Monitor signs of exhaustion, such as irritability, lack of focus, or physical fatigue. Regular self-check-ins and proactive adjustments help you maintain your well-being before reaching the breaking point.

➢ **Limit Exposure to Draining Influences:** Certain people, situations, or environments can sap your energy. Be mindful of your interactions and minimize exposure to negativity when possible. By protecting your mental space, you preserve the focus and resilience needed to stay aligned with your mission.

#builtlikeourancestors

Strategy

29 REST AND RESTORE

Be In The Know Prompts:

- **Know Your Value**
  Recognize that you are deserving of the time and care it takes to recharge. Prioritizing rest is an acknowledgment of your worth and a reminder that your well-being is as significant as the mission you're pursuing.

- **Know Your Limits**
  Understand your physical, emotional, and mental boundaries. Pushing past your limits without reprieve can lead to exhaustion, which ultimately diminishes your ability to make an impact. Awareness of when you're nearing burnout is key to preserving your strength.

- **Know the Endgame**
  Keep your long-term vision in mind. Rest isn't a diversion from your goals; it's a deliberate step that ensures you have the energy to see them through. By recharging now, you maintain the stamina needed for the entirety of your journey.

> ***Strategic Focus***
> In high-stakes situations, resilience isn't just about pushing forward; it's about knowing when to pause. "Rest and Restore" doesn't mean retreat. It's an intentional act of self-preservation that empowers you to continue fighting with clarity and purpose. By embracing rest as a strategic tool, you ensure that your energy is replenished and that you can show up fully, ready to face challenges with renewed power.

#builtlikeourancestors

This approach frames rest as an integral part of your resilience strategy, encouraging you to see it not as a setback but as a means of fortifying your strength for the battles ahead.

Actions:

1. **Establish Energy-Renewing Boundaries**

    ✓ Identify the situations, commitments, or relationships that drain your energy and set firm boundaries to protect yourself. By saying no to what depletes you, you create space for what truly restores and strengthens you.

    ✓ *Reflect: How can these boundaries enhance your effectiveness? What is one specific boundary you can establish today to safeguard your energy?*

2. **Carve Out Dedicated Time for Restorative Practices**

    ✓ Make rest a deliberate and non-negotiable part of your routine. Prioritize activities that recharge you, whether through solitude, time in nature, creative pursuits, or connection with loved ones. Treat these moments as essential investments in your well-being.

    ✓ *Reflect: What practices help you feel most renewed? How can you weave these moments into your life consistently and intentionally?*

#theartofstrategicresistance

3. **Conduct Regular Self-Assessments**

   ✓ Pause periodically to check in with yourself. Evaluate your energy levels, acknowledge your needs, and give yourself permission to adjust your pace when necessary. Regular self-assessment allows you to stay attuned to signs of burnout and proactively address them.

   ✓ *Reflect: What signals indicate that it's time for restoration? How can you incorporate self-assessments into your routine to stay grounded and resilient?*

Protective Strategies:

   ➤ **Champion Your Well-Being:** Prioritize your well-being as a cornerstone of your resilience. True strength lies not just in action but in knowing when to pause and recharge. Honor this as a vital part of sustaining your mission.

   ➤ **Reframe Rest as Resistance:** Recognize rest as a powerful act of resistance against burnout and fatigue. Choosing to refuel is a declaration of your commitment to the journey, ensuring you remain strong and purposeful.

   ➤ **Stand Firm in Your Worth:** Embrace the belief that your well-being deserves time and care. By honoring your need for restoration, you reclaim the power to decide how and when to engage, reinforcing your agency and value.

The strategies you've explored are more than just tools. They're a compass to guide you through high-stakes moments with clarity, confidence, and conviction. They serve as a reminder of your inherent power: the power to respond thoughtfully, to lead with purpose, to safeguard what matters, and to create meaningful, lasting impact.

This isn't about adhering to a rigid formula. It's about intentionally choosing your path, honoring your emotions, and aligning your actions with your deepest values and purpose. Some strategies may resonate with you immediately; others may reveal their significance more profoundly as your journey unfolds.

Remember:

- ✓ **Your Power is Multifaceted:** Whether you move with quiet determination or bold defiance, your power lies in how you show up, for yourself and for others.

- ✓ **Every Choice is an Opportunity:** Each decision you make shapes your future. Lead with awareness, act with integrity, and take deliberate steps toward building the world you envision.

- ✓ **You Are Never Alone:** In moments when the stakes feel highest, draw strength from the resilience of those who came before you and the community that stands with you today.

As you carry these strategies forward, let them guide not just moments of challenge but your everyday journey. Use them to amplify your voice, fortify your resolve and remind yourself of the immense power you hold to lead with purpose and courage.

#theartofstrategicresistance

Take the Next Step: Expand Your Journey

Your Tactical Guide is meant to grow with you, evolving as you navigate new challenges and opportunities. To support your continued growth, we've developed additional tools and resources designed to help you amplify your impact and deepen your practice of strategic resistance.

Visit **www.theartofstrategicresistance.com** to:

➢ Purchase The Art of Strategic Resistance Battle Planner: This companion tool is designed to help you map your strategies, stay organized, and track your progress with intention.

➢ Download Exclusive Resources: Access materials that complement this guide, offering ongoing support and practical insights to empower your journey.

These tools are your next steps toward building a legacy, one that honors the past, strengthens the present, and empowers the future. Take action now to keep the momentum alive and the movement thriving.

As we move forward, it's time to focus on what comes next: creating a legacy, staying true to your values, and continuing to rise with purpose and determination.

#builtlikeourancestors

CHAPTER 4

ANCESTRAL LEGACY AND FORWARD VISION

We began this journey with an Ode to Our Ancestors, honoring those who paved the way with resilience, strength, and vision. They endured and rose against forces designed to hold them back, yet they moved forward with unwavering spirit, carving a path that would one day lead to us. Their stories are the foundation upon which we stand, the legacy we carry forward.

Now, as we navigate these high-stakes times, we must remember that our role is not just to look back but also to look ahead. We are not only inheritors of a legacy. We are ancestors in the making for generations yet to come. One day, we will be the stories that our children, grandchildren, and their descendants look to for guidance and strength. They will speak of us as we speak of those who came before, and they will draw inspiration from the choices we make now, in these moments of strategic resistance.

They will remember us as the ones who stood firm in times of uncertainty, who pushed forward even when the path was unsteady, and who refused to let our voices be diminished. The future will honor us not only for what we achieved but for how we lived, how we resisted, how we rose, and how we loved.

We are Built Like Our Ancestors, carrying both their unyielding strength and the weight of a future they could scarcely envision.

This is our call: to live as the kind of ancestors we would be proud to have. To live, resist, and rise with the understanding that the future is watching. That those yet unborn will look to us as their foundation, their proof that strength and resilience flow through their bloodline. Every choice we make today, every act of courage, and every stand we take as part of Strategic Resistance adds another layer to the legacy we leave behind.

Let us be the ancestors whose names evoke strength and determination, whose memory inspires courage, and whose actions ripple forward with purpose and power.

#builtlikeourancestors

We must embrace this responsibility fully. We are here to do more than survive; we are here to define what survival and success mean for those who come after us. The fight for justice, freedom, and dignity does not end with us. It begins anew with every generation. What we build today, the blueprint, the Tactical Guide, the strategies of resistance, lays the foundation for a future we may never see but remain undeniably part of.

As you carry this Tactical Guide forward, let it remind you of your place in a long, unbroken line of resilience and power. This isn't just a guide; it's a blueprint for living and leading in ways that ensure we will be the ancestors our descendants honor with pride and gratitude.

This moment, this high-stakes journey, will one day become part of someone else's story, just as the past has shaped yours. So, stand tall. Move forward. And remember, you are not only living for yourself but for the generations who will one day look to you as a guide, a pillar, a source of inspiration.

We are Built Like Our Ancestors

We are the architects of the future, shaping it not only for ourselves but for the generations yet to come. In this shared mission, we stand shoulder to shoulder with those who came before us, honoring their fight while paving the way for those who will follow. This is our moment, to rise, to resist, and to embrace our destiny as the ancestors we are called to be.

#theartofstrategicresistance

CHAPTER 5

UNYIELDING LEGACY

Built Like Our Ancestors is more than a declaration or a catchy phrase. It is a truth that informs every step we take. It is our collective war cry, a reminder that the legacy of resilience and brilliance we inherit is not just to be celebrated but to be carried forward with intention, pride, and purpose.

Our ancestors faced unimaginable trials, yet they held steadfast to their vision, their dignity, and their fight for a future they believed in. Their strength flows through us, grounding us and preparing us for the high-stakes challenges we face today. They carved a path for us; not only to survive but to rise and thrive. Now, it is our charge to become the ancestors that future generations will look to when their own battles emerge.

This Tactical Guide is yours: to own, to use, and to pass forward. With every act of courage and every moment of resistance, you are building a legacy that will empower those who come after you. By declaring our power, we commit to embodying the same resilience and vision that those before us carried with unwavering faith.

This is the art of strategic resistance; not just a collection of strategies but a generational mission. It is an enduring legacy of strength and unyielding conviction. Use it wisely, with pride, and with the knowledge that you, too, are Built Like Our Ancestors. Because of you, future generations will know their own power. This is your legacy, your contribution, and your commitment to shaping the world you envision.

Together, we rise, we build, and we pass on the strength we've inherited, fortified by the past, ready for today, and creating the future.

#builtlikeourancestors

We are Built Like Our Ancestors!

A Legacy in Motion: Keep the Resistance Alive

But this isn't the end. It's the beginning of something much larger. Something meant to grow with each of us who choose to embrace this Tactical Guide and make it a part of who we are. We are the ancestors of tomorrow. Every action we take, every moment we resist, and every time we stand firm, we're laying the groundwork for those who will follow in our footsteps. They will look back and say, They didn't wait. They chose to act. They understood what was at stake.

You've been equipped with strategies born from a lineage of resilience, crafted to help you navigate a world that often feels like it's working against us. But remember, this Tactical Guide is only as powerful as the effort you put into it. This isn't a guide to read once and set aside. It's a living, breathing playbook meant to move with you. Bring it into the rooms where your voice is needed, into the spaces where your strength matters, and into the conversations where truth demands to be spoken.

Use these strategies whenever you need them, in the quiet moments when doubt creeps in and in the pivotal battles that define your journey. Let them be your armor and your fuel, knowing they're here for you again and again, no matter what life brings. As you grow, let these strategies grow with you. Adapt them, refine them, and make them your own.

And then, pass them on.

Don't keep this wisdom to yourself. Share it. Teach it. Gift it. Empower those around you to carry their own Tactical Guides, to stand stronger, speak louder, and understand they are never alone in this fight. This movement needs all of us. It needs to ripple beyond these pages, living in the hearts and actions of those willing to fight for something greater.

#theartofstrategicresistance

We are Built Like Our Ancestors, but this is our time. Now we take their spirit, their strength, and their legacy forward. Together, we'll transform this Tactical Guide into a way of life, a way to keep moving, keep resisting, and keep building a future our children and their children will thank us for.

Ancestral legacy loading ...

#builtlikeourancestors

CHAPTER 6

BUILT LIKE MY ANCESTORS: A BATTLE CRY FOR THE AGES

Built Like My Ancestors: A Battle Cry for the Ages

I am Built Like My Ancestors,
Bold, unbreakable, and here with purpose.
I carry the fire of those who came before, unyielding, unafraid, unforgotten.
Girded with grit and grace, unwavering in pride, vision, and foresight.
I am my ancestors' wildest dream, and their strength flows through my veins.
I will stand where others fall, speak where silence is imposed, resist where oppression reigns.
My voice is my weapon, my mind is my shield, my spirit is my battle plan.
I will not just endure,
I will rise, reclaim, and create.
For my children, for their children, and for every voice waiting to break free,
For those yet to come, for the ones who watch, for those who seek a path,
Their spirit flows through me, a fire that can't be quenched, a light that won't go dim.
I will leave a legacy of courage, a trail of resilience, and a world that knows our power.
Built Like My Ancestors, I am not just a dream,
I AM THE REVOLUTION.
And as I stand, fight, and rise, they will know,
I am Built Like My Ancestors!

#builtlikeourancestors

Epilogue

Join the Movement

I've mentioned a couple of times in this book the quote, "I belong everywhere I am, but I don't belong everywhere." It means that every room that I step into, I belong there; I deserve to be there. But not every room deserves my presence.

That's the motto I live by and my guiding principle for deciding where to show up, how and when to take action and with whom to share my presence. This same principle is instructive for the opposite – where not to show up, how and when not to take action and with whom to not share my presence.

This is the blueprint for my strategic resistance battle plan.

The strategies in this book have been designed to help you creating your guiding principles. But just as easily as anything else, you could choose to read this book, do nothing, and move on.

Or as a warrior, you could choose to join the movement to not only be your ancestors' wildest dreams but to take control of your life, living, and legacy and become your descendant's wildest dreams.

The choice is yours.

#theartofstrategicresistance

Visit **www.theartofstrategicresistance.com** for more resources and to learn more about what you can do to be part of the movement.

Together, we can create change.

We are Built Like Our Ancestors!

#builtlikeourancestors

Acknowledgments

To my parents, Sonia, and Teddy, for being the first and brightest lights of my life. Thank you for instilling in me the courage to dream, the strength to fight, and the confidence to believe that I could do anything I set my mind to. Your unwavering love, constant encouragement, and shining examples of character and integrity have shaped every part of who I am. You are my greatest cheerleaders, and I carry your lessons with me always.

To my husband, John, my steady anchor in every storm. Thank you for being my solid ground, my safe space, and my silent partner in every dream I pursue. Your calm, unwavering support allows me the freedom to create, to be bold, and to move forward without fear. I am grateful for the love and stability you provide, which keeps me centered even when I'm all over the place.

To my sister Lisa René, my confidante, my sounding board, and my constant. Thank you for always having my back, for calling me out and calling me up, and for being both my thermometer and thermostat. Your belief in me, your fierce loyalty, and your relentless encouragement never let me forget who I am or what I'm capable of. You're always there, cheering me on, lifting me up, and giving me ideas that push me to be better. I couldn't do this without you.

To my son, Jordan, my muse, and my inspiration since the day you were born. You are the reason I strive to be my best and to show up with

#theartofstrategicresistance

courage, integrity, and strength every day. My greatest hope is to make you proud; to be the best mom I can be in this life, and the ancestor you'll look back on with pride and to lay a foundation that reflects the legacy you deserve. You remind me every day of what it means to live with intention and purpose.

To my IRIE family, your unwavering love and support have been my refuge and my motivation. I want to especially acknowledge Toni Nicole, Chloé, and Danielle for sparking the fire that became this book. Your stories, your strength, and your brilliance inspired me to create a timeless resource that honors our ancestors and empowers future generations.

To Dr. Renée Baker, my ride-or-die, my safe space, my true friend. Thank you for always having my back, for being the place where I can vent, cry, dream, and celebrate (all in the same conversation - LOL), and for constantly holding space for me with love and authenticity. Your friendship is a gift I treasure deeply.

To my friend Precious Williams. Thank you for always speaking my name. Your unprompted kindness, your belief in me and my work, and your constant support mean more than words can express. You amplify my light without expectation, and I am endlessly grateful for you.

Finally, to every person who has ever encouraged, supported, or believed in me, thank you. This work is a reflection of all the love, strength, and inspiration you've poured into me. Together, we are creating a legacy that will endure.

#builtlikeourancestors

About the Author

Kelly Charles-Collins, Esq., MBA

Kelly Charles-Collins is a high-stakes communications expert, strategist, award-winning speaker, and author, celebrated for empowering leaders, teams, and speakers with the skills to communicate powerfully, lead confidently, and influence meaningful outcomes.

With over two decades of experience as an employment law trial lawyer, mediator, arbitrator, and educator, Kelly has developed a profound understanding of high-pressure environments. This unique background enables her to equip clients with world-class tools to excel in public speaking, presentation design and delivery, and influence-building. Her training focuses on empowering corporate teams, women leaders, and speakers to communicate with clarity, confidence, and credibility, shifting perspectives and amplifying authority.

An award-winning TEDx speaker and keynote speaker, Kelly is also the author of several influential books, including Convo Catalyst: The Humanistic Guide to Ignite Dialogue, Shift Perspectives & Cultivate Change, Conversations Change Things: The 'PER'fect Framework for Courageous Conversations, and Unapologetic AF: 34 Ways to Unleash Your Inner Badass. Her expertise has been featured on ABC, CBS, and NBC, and her thought leadership has appeared in Forbes, Fast Company, and Authority Magazine. Kelly is a two-time recipient

#theartofstrategicresistance

of the Most Inclusive HR Influencer Award, was named 2nd in the Women Changing the World Entrepreneur of the Year Award and was recognized as a Top Public Speaking Voice on LinkedIn.

Kelly's ultimate mission is to foster environments where communication elevates both the individual and the collective, sparking transformation, inspiring action, and driving change. Her signature blend of practical skill-building, strategic insight, and emotional intelligence ensures that her clients don't just communicate, they command the room and create lasting impact.

Kelly is available for keynotes, fireside chats, media interviews, leadership development training and team building. To learn more about how you and Kelly can work together, visit the websites below or email kelly@kellycharlescollins.com.

CONNECT WITH KELLY:
www.kellycharlescollins.com
www.bookkellycc.com
www.linkedin.com/in/kellycharlescollins
www.youtube.com/@kellycharlescollins

#builtlikeourancestors

Strategy Index

Building Strength and Allies
    Amplify Your Strengths, 46, 49, 141-143
    Command the Room, 46, 49, 81, 96
    Develop Your Playbook, 46, 49, 77
    Engage the Disengaged, 46, 49, 109
    Rallying Your Allies
        and Advocates, 46, 49, 89
    Organize, Mobilize,
        Engage, 46, 49, 93, 95

Grounding and Gaining Clarity
    Devise Your Strategy, 46, 49, 53-54
    Position for Power, 46, 49, 73
    Scout the Terrain, 46, 49, 65-66
    Speak with Purpose, 46, 49, 85-86
    Stand Your Ground, 46, 49, 61
    Trust Your Instincts, 46, 49, 151, 153

Navigating and Evolving
    Adapt and Advance, 46, 50, 137-139
    Engage the Opposition, 46, 50, 99
    Leverage and
        Capitalize, 46, 50, 131, 133

Ponder & Deliberate, 46, 50, 57-58
Review and Recalibrate, 46, 50, 147

Protecting and Sustaining
    Focus on the Endgame, 46, 50-51, 159
    Fortify Your Resolve, 46, 51, 55, 163, 179
    Persist and Persevere, 46, 51, 167, 168
    Protect Your Energy, 3, 46, 51, 171, 173
    Rest and Restore, 46, 51, 175-176
    Wield Strategic Silence, 46, 51, 155

Taking Action with Conviction
    Challenge with
        Conviction, 46, 50, 113-114
    Demand Accountability, 46, 50, 106, 123
    Disrupt Expectations, 43, 46, 50, 119-121
    Execute with Precision, 46, 50, 51, 127
    Exploit the Gap, 46, 50, 70
    Speak Truth to Power, 46, 49, 50, 103

#theartofstrategicresistance

www.ingramcontent.com/pod-product-compliance
Lightning Source LLC
Chambersburg PA
CBHW062040220426
43662CB00010B/1583